The Ghost of Stalin

Jean-Paul Sartre

The Ghost of Stalin

TRANSLATED FROM THE FRENCH

BY MARTHA H. FLETCHER

with the assistance of John R. Kleinschmidt

GEORGE BRAZILLER / *New York*

This essay, Jean-Paul Sartre's protest against the Soviet intervention in Hungary in 1956, first appeared in a series of articles in LES TEMPS MODERNES, Nos. 129, 130, 131 (November, December, 1956–January, 1957).

For information, address the publisher:
George Braziller, Inc.
One Park Avenue
New York, New York 10016

Library of Congress Catalog Card Number: 67–19872

Printed in the United States of America

The Ghost of Stalin

I have received many letters recently. Among the questions asked me are two recurring from very diverse pens, to which I think it is useful to respond publicly.

"BY WHAT RIGHT? . . ."

This one addresses itself, over my head, to *all* Frenchmen who condemn the Soviet intervention: "By what right? In the name of what principle? Of what philosophy? Of yours, doubtlessly. Then you should know that it commits (*engage*) only you."

Some readers will be surprised, I know, that one requires philosophical references to permit them to detest this slaughter. However, if they reflect, I think they will find the question proper. Some Communists have objected and, moreover, Mr. Denis de Rougement: it must not be for the same reasons. The game is so complex, in this affair, that it is necessary to announce one's color and one's stakes. The proof of this is that a provisional distinction has been hastily made: the Left condemns the Suez affair and that of Budapest; the Right that of Budapest only; *L'Humanité* that of Suez. In truth, the links between the two massacres—in the midst of a world situation where everything depends on everything—don't seem to be

* A Glossary of essential names and terms will be found on pp. 143–148.

1

particularly close: the Hungarian insurrection surprised the Russians, the Suez attack had been arranged for several months. It's possible that our great politicians precipitated the landing, in spite of the advice of generals, "to take advantage of the U.S.S.R.'s difficulties in Central Europe." I think they are stupid enough, in fact, not to have understood that it had the strongest army in the world, that it could crush Hungary and throw 200,000 men into Suez, that its difficulties are not of a military order and that it would be only too content to be able to raise its great voice loudly enough to cover the death-rattle of Budapest; but all that doesn't lead anywhere. Since then, Mr. Mollet and *L'Huma* have made the most touching attempts to establish a profound tie between these disparate events. The former declares: "The Hungarians in Budapest, the French in Egypt, have come up against the same arms,"[1] and the latter: "The same fascists demolished Port Said and hanged the Hungarian workers." Let them talk; the sad truth is that the French Left can define itself today only by a double refusal.

Nevertheless these two undertakings have this in common, that they are both political in nature and that they cannot be appraised without taking into account the objectives to be obtained and the interests to be defended, in short without passing a *political* judgment whose repercussions can be only political.

I know Mr. De Rougement: he's a gentle man, well brought up and, into the bargain, a Swiss; the military prestige of France doesn't dazzle him. It seems probable then that this "European" considered the Suez affair as a rather sinister blunder; however, he didn't say anything. On Budapest, he

---

[1] The French must also have run up against French arms. And English. It is not so long ago that we were Nasser's armaments suppliers.

2

has expressed himself abundantly. It's because he's anticommunist: by taste, by role, by profession. Now, his condemnation remains purely and simply *moral*: he rises up in the name of international law. It's his silence which is political. Or rather this mixture of muteness and declamations. He won't touch the hands of the Communist intellectuals: ah, there, you think, is a very idealistic reaction. But no; it *gives itself* an appearance of idealism, but one will discover its real significance if one considers that De Rougement would shake Guy Mollet's hand without any disgust. Here's what one of my correspondents says to me: "Only they, the advocates of absolute non-violence are able to judge." Which means: only they who put the refusal to spill blood above everything else have the right to take a *moral* position. Of course. But it's precisely because they condemn *political* action a priori. By the same token the Soviet and French leaders have the right to challenge them: these moralists didn't defend France against Hitler, they didn't resist under the occupation, or, if they did, they contradicted their own principles. Politics is necessary and no one can get mixed up in it—be it the ordinary citizen who votes for a party every four years—if he doesn't accept at the outset that violence, in some cases, is the lesser evil. I summarize the letter of a progressive who puts the question rather clearly: "You're not Christian, the Communists aren't either; can you say to them: Thou shalt not kill? No more than they, do you believe in the virtues of passive resistance, conscientious objection, absolute pacifism: Can you reproach them for their violence? You consider—as they do—the Rights of Man and of the Citizen as abstract principles of the bourgeois Republic: Can you condemn the Marxists in the name of outworn guarantees which have never prevented misery nor exploitation?"

He's right: at worst, the *moral* stance covers up a politi-

3

cian's operation; at best, it doesn't come to grips with the facts, the moralist is out of it. But politics, any politics, is an action conducted in common by some men against other men. Based on convergences or divergences of interests, the relations of solidarity like the relations of combat and hostility define a total attitude of man towards man, the immediate objectives are clarified by long-run objectives, the praxis is controlled by the value judgments which it engenders and which are indistinguishable from factual judgments;[1] thus true politics contains within it implicitly, it's own moral appraisal. And the best way to judge *totally* the undertaking of a government or party is to judge it *politically*. By that I don't claim that just any of the French parties has the right to pass judgment on just any other. For more than a century, under forms which change in the course of history, only one movement impels the exploited to claim for themselves and for all the possibility of being men fully and totally; only one movement reveals society itself in all its reality and defines the bourgeoisie by exploitation when all the others are making it the universal class; only one produces, through action and by means of it, an ideology which allows it to understand itself and to understand the others: this is the socialist movement taken as a whole. It is the absolute judge of all the others because the exploited encounter exploitation and the class struggle as their reality and as the truth of bourgeois societies: it sees the inner meaning of maneuvers and operations because it can't help but relate them to the

---

[1] On August 10, 1792, after the victory of the uprising, the crowds invade the Tuileries; several persons try to pillage, they are hanged. This condemnation is a political act in that it is first of all concerned with the effect which these thefts would produce on the adversary and with the advantage which the counterrevolutionary propaganda would get from them if they remained unpunished. But it is inseparable from certain values of the people: disgust with royal luxury and the consequent refusal to benefit from it, the revolutionary requirement of purity, etc.

fundamental structures of history, because it is the movement of man in the process of making himself. The other parties believe that man is already made and that he is the abstract subject of bourgeois property, a morose angel whose needs are all gratified. They cover up exploitation and break up the class struggle into sporadic and individual conflicts; their ideologists and historians look for the meaning of history everywhere, except where it is. Hence, they don't have the means for understanding the action of the exploited classes nor for judging it; they take away from themselves even the power of judging themselves since they refuse to know the truth of what they do. To appraise a political undertaking, socialism is the ultimate reference: it understands Mr. Laniel who doesn't understand himself. Naturally, this movement would be incapable of having abstract principles or an a priori program: it is in perpetual metamorphosis like production itself, like the relationships of force, in a word, like history. It would be absurd to refer to Blanqui and even to Guesde in order to appraise what's happening today; and if one "returns" to Leninism, closer to us, still alive, it must be rethought in terms of a situation which it couldn't foresee. But the very development of socialism, the principles it sets up by its daily praxis, which flow from the masses themselves, which it picks up and makes precise in its propaganda, the condemnation which it levels daily against its adversaries, its real action, the concrete relation which ties its immediate objectives to its long-range goals, in short the actual totality of its movement offers us lights to clarify all enterprises and its own first of all. Its appraisals are correct: the errors, the knowledge gaps, the momentary weaknesses in no way change that. History has not retained Mr. Thiers' version of the 1848 massacres or of the Commune: it has held with the judgment of the people, and the interpretation of Marx and De Lissagaray. It is socialism, itself, which can and must appraise the action of socialist Guy Mollet, and that of socialist Russia.

These conclusions would cause us to slip into idealism if we were to leave it at that; for socialism is never simple: it splits up and opposes itself. In our country, for example, the two great parties of the workers, in spite of a few too-brief armistices, have been fighting each other since the Congress of Tours: they differ by their recruitment, by the unions they support as well as by their electoral clientele, by the interests they represent, by their political action, by their programs, by ideology, and by the value judgments which, born of their praxis, turn back on it to check on it or to correct it. It would be pointless to rely on the actual politics of one or the other: we would be quickly brought, like the militants, to swallow Suez or Budapest, you pick one, if not out of conviction at least out of loyalty. It would be naïve to seek in them a community of principles which they don't have and to base the appraisal of their behavior on some kind of universal socialism which would boil down, in the final count, to an idealistic eclecticism. It would be presumptuous and useless to create, by ourselves, for the needs of the cause, an abstract theory which we would call "true" socialism, or "pure" Marxism; one would quite rightly respond to us, as does my correspondent: "That's *your* philosophy, nobody shares it." One has to decide, however: our judgment on the Egyptian affair and on that of Hungary judges us and defines us. We will say then, to begin with, that communism seems to us, in spite of everything, like the only movement which still bears within itself the positive potential of socialism's chances. But, in the present phase of socialist construction, violent contradictions are splitting the U.S.S.R. and the Peoples Democracies, setting the latter against the former, throwing the Western C.P.s into the midst of crisis. At the origin of these conflicts are the economic transformations of the East and the upheavals which accompany them. This great movement of organization and disorganization, of integration and expansion, reveals itself at the level of the leaders, by completely contradictory undertakings—whether they be undertaken simultaneously by groups which oppose each other or whether they represent the ever widening oscillations of a leadership united but incapable of going beyond the objective contradictions, endlessly tossed between Charybdis and Scylla —and by extraordinary procrastinations. If they take part in this conflict, the men of the Left must serve a policy *here* which is constantly re-examined and combatted *there,* which frankly accepts the metamorphosis in progress in order to be able to direct it and to complete it without too much cost. As to what concerns me and to reply to my correspondent, I must determine in what political perspectives military action could indeed appear the lesser evil. It will then be necessary that the appraisal itself of these perspectives bring out in its broad lines the socialist policy in the name of which I made the assessment, the only one which is at once requisite with and sustained by reality.

So many precautions aren't necessary to judge Mr. Guy Mollet: he has never claimed to serve the cause of socialism. In all truth, he doesn't intend anything at all. It's easy, then, to appraise his politics, that is to say, to measure the distance between the decisions he takes and the living reality of the masses whom he represents and who voted for him. Mr. Duverger has remarkably demonstrated that anticommunism and the slow degradation of the S.F.I.O. Party perpetually obligates its parliamentary group to choose between opposition and betrayal. Mr. Mollet has thrown himself into betrayal; he splashes about in it comfortably. I don't know anyone in history who has betrayed so many people at once.

First, his allies: Before even forming his government, he sacrificed Mr. Mendès-France to the demands of the M.R.P.

Then, his electors: They had carried him to power because he had promised to make peace. Now, here they are with two conflicts on their hands.

And then, all Frenchmen, in general: He made the blood of soldiers flow *for nothing*, he disorganized the French economy by a criminal and imbecilic adventure, and he succeeded in lining up the United Nations unanimously against our country. He has shown to everyone a contemptible France in which we refuse to recognize ourselves: cruel against the weak and cowardly before the strong.

Finally, and above all—since this is what concerns us—*he has betrayed his Party*. No one asked him to transform by a stroke of the pen the fatherland of Mr. Boussac into a socialist country. At least he could negotiate with the Algerians, undertake reforms in France, build housing. But no; this successor of Jaurès must be myopic: he confuses the interests of the nation with those of Mr. Borgeaud, he sends the poor to war to defend colonialism and the big Companies; he puts at the service of the capitalists the power that the support of the wage earners gives him, he ruins at one fell swoop the pacifist traditions of his party by rashly throwing himself into a war of aggression. And what a war! An insidious propaganda ceaselessly murmurs in our ears: "Nasser the dictator! Nasser the dictator!" in order to persuade us that we are liberating Egypt from a tyrant. Nonsense! Our planes have dropped their bombs on miserable peasants wasting away from chronic famine. Nasser, in nationalizing the canal, was obeying the popular

will: with these new resources he would have built a dam, irrigated, and increased the productivity of the Egyptian earth.[1]
Mollet, in the name of the Company, caused lightning to fall
on these insolent fellahs: let them die of poverty as long as the
Suez stockholders get their dividends. At the same time, he
places the militants before a dilemma: leave the Party or publicly support an undertaking which they profoundly condemn.
Some leave. Those who remain, out of loyalty to socialism, he
makes bedfellows of the British Conservatives; he forces them
to suffer the scorn of the Laborites, their natural allies, and,
worse still, the applause of Mr. Duchet. This political wheel
nursed the hypocritical illusion of pulling along a rightist majority to support a leftist policy: it's the illusion of all traitors,
at the start. He has recovered today: he's a traitor without illusions. But this experience will cost his Party dear: colonialist, imperialist and bellicose, our War Lord knowingly carries
out a rightist policy with a rightist majority. On all the charts,
the Right wins: it attains its objectives and socialism disqualifies itself. Mr. Mollet will be given the time to put into operation all the unpopular measures which his faults make inevitable; then the Right will prick this windbag and take power to
unanimous applause. At this moment, fascism will be very
near and the S.F.I.O. liquidated.

The "Budapest affair" is an entirely different matter and the
questions asked are of a different scope. The Government of
the U.S.S.R., if it is to be believed, intervened in Hungary to

---

[1] That he is a dictator is certain. So what? An Egyptian Communist told
me: "Nasser has imprisoned my two brothers and all my friends. Which
is as much as telling you that I hardly like him. But, in this Suez affair,
he has all the people behind him. And if the historical circumstances had
allowed a popular front to take power, that government would have acted
in the same way."

save the foundations of socialization there; it decided on this intervention the day when the magnitude of the counterrevolutionary disturbances had made it inevitable.

That's why one of my correspondents concludes: "You claim to be a socialist; then thank the Soviets for having safeguarded, even by violence, Hungarian socialism."

In sum, I am reproached with isolating these massacres, considering them by themselves without taking into account the historical content, the necessities, the goal. Mollet, at Port Said, was killing to defend the interests of capitalism: it's for this reason and in this perspective that the Anglo-French landing was to be condemned. But if one approves defensive wars, wars of liberation, the Maquis, the uprising of oppressed classes, in brief, if, in certain cases, one accepts violence, how does one reject it when socialist construction is at stake, when armed fascists are hanging Party militants, when the West is preparing to reap the harvest of counterrevolution. To save the conquests of the proletariat in Hungary is, at the same time, to protect them in all the Peoples Democracies and, in the final count, in the U.S.S.R. itself: the Red Army takes up and continues in Hungary—with means of a somewhat greater magnitude—what the workers and sailors of Saint Petersburg began in October, 1917; if socialism tolerates the cannon shots of the battleship *Aurora*, why would it condemn those of Zhukov's tanks?

Such is the current argument in some progressive and communist circles: it's called Marxist. I think it's much older than Marx. It can be summarized thus: "What's necessary is necessary" (*"Faut ce qu'il faut"*). Each one expounds it according to the peculiar nuances of his sensibility. There are the courageous who smile gallantly: "Well, yes! There are some dead. So what? Do you even imagine the quantity of human lives that a world revolution costs! You have to get used to it, you see. You have to put up with these dead people: it's our duty." There are the overwhelmed who haven't shut their eyes since November 4 and who weep indiscriminately over the honest workers hanged by the fascists and over the innocent proletarians struck by a Soviet shell—a lost shell, of course. They speak to you tearfully of a "tragic dilemma" and of a "painful duty," but if you ask them: "But *you*? What is your own opinion on the events?" they move away hurriedly saying: "I? Well, I'm overwhelmed, simply overwhelmed." There are the jovial who laugh at others' anger: "But my good friend, don't get all worked up; you're just feeling cuckolded, that's all." They are sure of themselves: never will they believe themselves cuckolded, short of a million deaths. There are the aggressive: "Well, old man, it's lucky you weren't the head of the Hungarian government; you would be hanged by now, and Horthy would be in power." There are the impartial—usually progressives—who have learned to distrust their personal reactions: "One must judge sanely, cool-headedly, one must look ahead: socialism is an enormous event which is measured in the scale of centuries. In a few decades, no one will be sensitive any longer to the anecdotal aspect of the massacres, and their necessity, strained clear, will appear in its true light." There are the dialecticians who shrug their shoulders: "The Russians are all for world peace, and they hit out at Hungary like blind men? So? That proves there's one more contradiction in the process of socialization, it only has to be named." One of them writes me: "Why disassociate oneself from an action which is deplorable, certainly, but which is entirely justifiable if one admits for a moment, the moment of truth, that there exists today a new contradiction between socialism and peace, a contradiction which is not resolved by classical Marx-

11

ist doctrine?" And then there are my two correspondents: "In the name of what do you judge?" All of them are sheltering their discomfort behind this reasoning: socialism first; we'll kill if it's necessary to kill, and let the blood of the innocent victims fall back on the criminals who impelled them to revolt.

On one point we're in agreement: Part of the bloodshed does fall back on the Western governments, on Mr. Truman's government. You noble souls, tender souls who get so indignant today, in the columns of *Figaro Littéraire*, did you know that radios, subsidized or not by the United States, were daily inciting the Hungarians to rise up when the West had neither the means nor the intention of supporting them? But of course you knew it; it wasn't hidden from anyone and the bourgeois newspapers congratulated themselves on it. Did you protest? No, you approved of this propaganda or else you were thoughtless, self-centered, trifling above all and you were silent about the havoc it wrought. Well, now read in the bourgeois press (in *France-Soir*, for example, and in *L'Express*) the reports of special correspondents: you'll learn that the Hungarians are spitting on our flag. The people over there who considered these broadcasts to be pernicious and lying are joining today with those whom the broadcasts encouraged; you can go ahead and offer them your magnificent heavy hearts: they answer your outpourings with hatred.

That said, I consider the argument of the overwhelmed and of the grouches to be a striking sophism cunningly based on unproven assertions: it would be necessary to prove to us that socialism was lost without Zhukov's tanks. Now the facts which they report to us—true or false, in general more false than true—tell us simply that it was in danger. To take for granted that the Russian intervention saved socialism, is to take the U.S.S.R. off the hook: necessity obliges it to strike, it

12

re-establishes the situation, that's all—an objective disorder automatically set off conpensatory mechanisms. Nobody has been willing to understand, among these zealots, that the U.S.S.R. *defined by its acts* its own socialism and that which it counts on re-establishing in Hungary; nobody has dared to ask himself whether this military action, in reducing the internal relations of the socialist camp to relationships of force, hasn't more seriously harmed the cause being defended than would have free elections and neutralization; nobody has seen that the intervention *was the expression of a political policy*. To respond to my correspondents, it is necessary then to start afresh and begin at the beginning.

Let us concede for a moment that the intervention was unavoidable. Then it must be that the regular government recognized its impotency: after twelve years of absolute power, it had lost control over the masses and no longer represented them. Its isolation, the hatred borne it even in Communist ranks, these are the real reasons for its appeal to the Soviets. The foreign intervention appears then as the logical conclusion of an abstract and erroneous policy which was leading to economic catastrophe and which was to engender of itself the counterrevolution. In this case, we refuse to consider and to appraise separately the last link in this chain. The overindustrialization and the accelerated collectivization *were already criminal*: they carried within themselves *from the first day* the massacres of Budapest as their outcome. These massacres, if our right to condemn them at their moment and from the day they began is taken away from us, we will condemn from the first day of 1949, for they were already there, they fouled in advance all the moves of blind leaders. What does it matter, in fact, what a government thinks it is doing? What counts is what it does. And what was it doing? It was systematically

13

pushing an entire people to despair. Those who come to speak to us, eyes bulging, about the diabolical power of the fascists, I must compare to Mr. Burnham, the well-known specialist on anticommunism. I had quite a laugh reading his books. He showed prosperous workers, tied to the employers by a community of interests, by a reciprocity of respect; it was happiness. Then, suddenly, issuing forth from hell, a handful of Communists appeared, and incited discord everywhere. Nothing more was needed to throw a happy people into despair. I've found these same arguments from Communist writers: the only difference is that they didn't make me laugh. Well, no, to be just, there's another difference: in socialist countries the workers *are expected to have* a community of interests with the leaders. But if they have it, if they are well-fed and if the standard of living is rising, if they are conscious of working for themselves in working for all, can one believe that fascism can persuade them that they are dying of hunger? And if they don't have it, whose fault is it? I don't underestimate the role of the émigrés: I say that people don't willingly get themselves killed when they can avoid it. I say that fascist propaganda is not enough to throw them in a bare-handed assault against tanks, and that for one to rush to one's death one must no longer see in life anything but a prolonged agony. I will not have the impertinence to remind the Communist leaders of the motto of the silk weavers of Lyons: "Live working or die fighting." I know however that they think it splendid. And they're right. But what else were the Hungarian workers saying?

These workers get curiously on the nerves of some of our Stalinist intellectuals. There are some of them who have decided systematically to deny their existence, like this fine bastard who said to me yesterday: "Budapest? A detestable city,

14

nine hundred thousand petits bourgeois dug into their holes."[1]
Others, more enlightened, don't dream of denying that the
Hungarian proletariat exists, that it took part in the insurrection, elected workers' councils and decreed the general strike.
But precisely for that our "hard-liners" don't look kindly on
the proletariat. Already Mr. Stil has been hard at work: these
committees, these factory councils, huh? Do you know where
they come from, and who elected them? Oh, come on! They're
controlled by the fascists. In Budapest it's well-known. Kadar
strikingly contradicted him the next day by considering them
as the representatives of the working class and by agreeing to
negotiate with them.[2] But already the argument has got somewhere. And someone was grumbling the other day: "The
working class? Well, what about the working class? Do you
think it's infallible? Did it budge when Louis Bonaparte made
his coup d'état? Weren't there workers behind Mussolini, behind Hitler?" If I hadn't heard these remarks with my own
ears I wouldn't dare to repeat them. And, of course, one will
agree that the working class isn't infallible if one means by
that that no one is infallible, that the truth little by little establishes itself in a dialectical relationship between the masses
and the cadres, in the midst of errors, of costly faults, through
debates and sometimes conflicts. But we will refuse to follow
the Communists who denounce the errors of the proletariat
when they seek argumentative advantage from them in order
to put their Political Bureau in the right *come what may*. It's a
fine one, indeed, to denounce the errors of the masses when it
proclaimed in turn the guilt of Kostov, of Rajk, of Slansky, of
the "white blouse criminals," when it denied the existence of the
labor camps, when it proved that Tito was a fascist "in the

---

[1] It's known that Budapest has 1,700,000 inhabitants.
[2] It's true he dissolved them two weeks later.

15

scientific sense of the term"! I know what it will say, what its members say every day: "Faults have been committed, but . . ." Only one can no longer accept that "but." Faults have been committed. Period. Linger a bit on that, Mr. Fajon. Draw some conclusions from it for yourself and for your friends. This one, for example: that it is necessary to be modest, at present, very modest; that Mr. Khrushchev has revealed your lies to the whole world and that it is preferable to wait for a little while before beginning them again. Besides, you see, the Hungarian workers could have been mistaken *politically*— you're the ones who say it and I'm willing to admit it for the time being. But when they were saying: "We have too much work, we haven't enough to eat," they were the absolute measure of what was too much and what was not enough. By refusing to hear them, the Rakosis, the Gerös—these friends whom you are still defending in private—proved to them that the policy of the Party was false, that the bureaucratic apparatus underestimated the revolutionary force of the masses and took no account of their aspirations. It is their errors which made the working class understand that, *even in a socialist country*, it had the obligation to create its own machinery of defense.

Everything considered, the French Communists should be advised not to shout too loudly that the Soviet intervention could not be avoided. For this pious argument carries the most radical condemnation of everything that has been done in Hungary up to now. Tortures, trumped up confessions, fake trials, work camps: these instances of violence are unpardonable in any situation. One would have perhaps forgotten them later if they had been only the residue of a great upheaval of a society in the process of laying the bases of socialism. But when everything crumbles at once, when the whole populace ranges itself on the side of fascism to liquidate the regime, the

16

bases of socialism never existed. How heavy then weigh all of these crimes committed for nothing, all these useless sacrifices. The failure of the Stalinists shows in their true light this misery and terror which had no other future than final catastrophe.

But I don't entirely share the unwitting severity of our Stalinists. I recognize that the agricultural collectivization was magnificently flubbed, that industrialization remains a semi-failure. But through all that, the nationalization of industry has borne its fruits: a working class has been forged which wishes to defend socialism. And one would not have much difficulty in applying to the Hungarians these words of a Communist friend who is fond of the Poles: "In Poland the automobile industry produced bad autos and admirable workers." No, the consequences of Stalinism were not *inevitable*: what was needed was to de-Stalinize in time. If, in 1955, Nagy had been left in power, if even he had been called back at the beginning of October, 1956, the insurrection would have been avoided. What drove the population to despair was the explosive mixture, within the Party itself, of a still aggressive Stalinism and supporters of de-Stalinization; it was the hesitations, the about-faces, the procrastinations and the contradictions. Let's not forget that Khrushchev, in this same month of October, was landing at Warsaw while the Russian troops and Rokossovsky's Polish troops were marching on the capital: if, at that moment, Gerö had been in the place of Ochab, they would be proving to us that the Russian intervention was necessary in Poland, they would be talking to us of Polish fascism. Inversely, if Ochab had been Secretary General of the Hungarian C.P., *Pravda* would be extolling Hungarian-Soviet friendship and would offer it as an example to the countries of Central Europe. And, without a doubt, it will be said that Gerö is the product of Stalinism: it's true; but Ochab was too. No, the chips are not down once and for all, it's necessary to struggle. But if the effusion of blood could still have been avoided in those first two weeks of October, what tells us that it was unavoidable at the very moment it took place?

Those who take for granted the necessity of the Russian intervention, were seen to take a position immediately and without the least information. It isn't Hungary which interests them: it's the U.S.S.R. And their conviction is born from an act of faith: "*Since* the Red Army cannot shoot at workers without an absolute necessity, the Budapest massacre must have been necessary." For them, the socialist structure of the U.S.S.R. decides its relations with the surrounding socialist countries and these relations can be only socialist. Now, the Communist parties of the whole world, the Peace Movement, the Soviet leaders have a hundred times condemned the principle of military intervention and proclaimed the rights of people to self-determination. *Therefore* the Soviet Army did not really intervene, except against foreign agents: it gave help to an allied government and to the working classes, it saved the good Communists from massacre, fought the Trotskyite demons and the Arrow Cross, encouraged the masses to repel temptations. Of the cannon volleys there must be remembered only the brilliant flashes which illuminated an indecisive people and showed it its way; guided by the historical process, the shells chose the fascists and struck only them.

The catch is that the Army of Socialism spilled blood at least once without the least necessity: in Hungary, precisely, a few days earlier, at the time of its first intervention. When people fantasy about November 4, they entirely forget that night of October 23 when the Soviet command, on Gerö's appeal, agreed to throw its troops at the crowd. No one dares claim today that it was a question then of a "fascist putsch."

Even Mr. Waldeck-Rochet admits that the first disorders betrayed "a legitimate discontent" of the workers. This crowd, in the streets, gay and upset—less upset perhaps than gay—wasn't quite sure whether it was *demanding* Nagy's return or whether it *was celebrating it in advance.* The Central Committee hadn't decided anything yet but, in the eyes of the masses, its decision seemed in the bag: if it had been announced right away, calm would have been gradually re-established. Gerö, on his return from Belgrade, furious at being humiliated in front of Tito, conducted himself like a provocator: could he be unaware that by treating the demonstrators as rabble he would change the demonstration with one stroke into a riot? Who knows whether he didn't want to? Who fired the first shots? Demonstrators? Avos? Rakosists betting on the worst? No one knows. But what is very well known, on the other hand, is that Gerö leaped at the opportunity and that he called the Red Army to his aid. But, Gerö is only a supernumerary. Who will swallow the idea that the Russian leaders had to obey him? Couldn't they, on the contrary, show him he was a washout and advise him to take off? Called back during the night, Nagy had every chance to quiet the riot *if* the Russian troops hadn't been in such a hurry to fire.

Installed, protected by the Soviets, Janos Kadar doesn't hesitate today to speak of the crimes of Gerö and Rakosi. His protectors allow him to say it. Must one believe that their soldiers fired on the people on the appeal of a criminal and to cover up his errors? Better yet: Nagy never hid what he thought of the appeal to the Soviets. The responsibility for it was attributed to him and he fiercely defended himself: "It's," he said, "the Rakosist assassins who tried to smear me." Now, Kadar was part of the Government and never protested; if he resigned on November 2, it's for other reasons which we'll dis-

19

cuss further on. He is still working hard today at justifying the events of November 4, but he never brings up the 23rd of October. This is to denounce implicitly Gerö's step as a gratuitous crime to which the Russians made themselves accomplices. And the Soviet Government? What does it say about it? What do the Soviet writers say about it in the message which they sent to us? Nothing. Absolutely nothing. This first massacre so greatly embarrasses the editors of *L'Humanité*, of *France Nouvelle*, Messrs. Garaudy and Waldeck-Rochet, that they all act as if it hadn't existed.[1] The activity of the fascist commandos, the lynchings, the shift toward the Right, all the more or less elucidated facts which they make something of—it's *after October 24* that they took place; *it's the second intervention* which they are trying to justify. But, I won't tire of repeating: it is the first which must be thought of first; it is it which must be spoken of always. And, when the Stalinists try to prove to us that the second aggression was in-

---

[1] I must say that I heard, at the Peace Movement, a glib speaker with a vacant stare whom this first intervention had hardly moved. I had spoken about it before him and I had defied him to prove to me its necessity. He came to the rostrum and sought to take up the challenge: "The first intervention?" he said with a cosy air. "I admit that you trouble me greatly: I hadn't thought about it. But I tell myself, you see, that if the U.S.S.R., with all its tanks, all its cannons and all its soldiers, had been willing to throw the whole wad in the first time, there wouldn't have been a second."

It's true. And I concede even more to my challenger: if the U.S.S.R. had been willing to try out its atomic weapons on Budapest and on some workers' centers, the Soviet leaders would not be importuned today by the exasperating and tenacious resistance of Hungary; the Hungarian problem would be no more than a problem of resettlement. Moreover, the approximate figure given by Nehru, from the report of his ambassador is known: 25,000 dead. "25,000 Hungarian dead," my "cadre" would undoubtedly say, "what magnaminity. What! There were nine million to kill and the U.S.S.R. left 8,975,000 of them alive! Naturally, it will be necessary to deduct, a little later, those dead from hunger or from cold and those who are shot. But at the very most that wouldn't reach 100,000. And you get indignant?" It's necessary to respond to this idiot that you don't justify a massacre by the number of victims.

evitable, let us respond that, in this case, it is the first which necessitated it. O, sanctimonious ones who brag shamelessly of having killed to prevent a world war, when it's your first assassinations which risked bringing it on! You claim to have saved socialism: yes, on November 4. Or at least, that can be argued about; but when you were firing, during those October days, when the tanks of the Communist Army at the call of a Communist chief were massacring Communist workers, it was socialism itself that your bullets and your shells were blowing to pieces.

In politics, no action is unconditionally necessary. Even after the "shift toward the Right" of the Hungarian revolution, no one can hold armed repression as necessary unless it is in a certain perspective which assumes certain immediate and other longer range objectives, a certain technical relationship to these ends, certain values, a conception of man. No more is needed to understand that this perspective is the particular feature of certain groups, that it reflects their makeup and their interests. To declare that, in the Hungarian affair, respect for "non-interference" would have led to a world war, one must develop for himself a certain idea of the Peoples Democracies, of the capitalist West, of the relationship of forces, of the class struggle; one must, in terms of these hypotheses, have bet on a certain future; one must have defined a policy in terms of this future itself and of the revolutionary strength of the various proletariats. This implies that one has certain information at one's disposal and that one evaluates it in a certain manner, that is to say in terms of certain views held and of a certain culture. But this culture and these views define in their turn the men who made the political choice: they send us back to their deep-seated attitude vis-a-vis socialism and vis-a-vis man, hence to their training, to their interests, to the class or milieu which produced them. A propos of the Hungarian events, there is only one question to ask: For what men and in what political perspective was the Soviet intervention necessary? We will not be able to answer it without first trying—to the extent possible—to determine the nature, the composition, and the evolution of the insurrectional movement between October 24 and the morning of November 4.

The statements of Radio-Budapest and, recently, certain admissions of the Communist leaders allow two extreme positions to be set aside: even the Communists admit today that it was not a question of a simple fascist putsch; only the Trotskyists hold that the entire insurrection had a progressive character. The truth lies somewhere between these two equally gratuitous and schematic affirmations. Somewhere, but where? To find it, a Marxist analysis of the situation would be necessary: but we still lack the elements. Fajon, Garaudy, Waldeck-Rochet repeat in chorus: "Let's be Marxists!" But after a few catechistic banalities on prewar Hungary and on its evolution after 1945, they stop short. It's because they know nothing: the only thing left for them is to declaim on the class struggle; it seems that we "underestimate" it. Now the class struggle exists: it's the prime mover of history. But it must not become the "whipping boy" of the Political Bureau. You will be forced to admit it some day, you lazy, flip Marxists: a popular insurrection in a socialist country cannot fit into your schemata. And you know it so well that you run it into the ground: what you call "class struggle" in Hungary is the exploitation of the revolt by foreign capitalism. Your absurd reasoning reduces itself to a series of false equivalences: the cold war is only a form of the class struggle;[1] everything which just might serve

---

[1] It's true, without any doubt. But it's false as soon as you speak of it because of your thought defects, your unconscious habits, your crude

22

the Western bloc is by definition counterrevolutionary: now, the Hungarian insurrection—whatever its goals, factors, agents—objectively plays the game of capitalist imperialism. Therefore it's a counterrevolution. They underestimate the class struggle, these intractable Hungarians who detest the tyranny of the Rakosists; they underestimate the class struggle, these national Communists who wish to establish true socialist relations between the U.S.S.R. and Hungary. And hunger? And the chronic fatigue of the workers? These needs push the underestimation so far that they make productivity drop off and sabotage socialist planning. But tell me, this Rakosi, in fact, wasn't he underestimating a bit, he who got you all into the soup? Couldn't he be an American agent by chance? And you who know the power of the Right, you who live in the midst of reactionary polemicists—mean, wily, quick to high-light your weaknesses—aren't you underestimating the class struggle when you serve us up the most stupid concoctions, when you make all France laugh at you, when you calmly censor in your newspapers the news which is lying around everywhere? When Mr. Stil courageously writes that Budapest has found its smile again and when Mr. Nehru, citing his ambassador's report, declares that the appearance of this city is "heartbreaking," who, in your opinion, is making the better anticommunist propaganda? Mr. Nehru or the editor-in-chief of *L'Humanité*? Couldn't you be, you too, a bit, just a little bit counterrevolutionary? Class struggle: these two words which designate a shifting and complex reality, always present, often difficult to figure out, you twist them to mean "the hand of Uncle Sam" and by that token you stoop to the level of an

___

dogmatism. Where have you made a study of this new reality, *the bloc*? Where have you shown what the class struggle becomes in the perspective of this immense conglomeration undermined by its perpetual contradictions?

idiotic Right which looks in all strikes for "the hand of Moscow." Those who don't immediately discern American parachutists in the middle of this poor and indignant crowd, you call petits bourgeois. Really, this slander is astonishing! The Communist intellectuals, what are they then, if not petits bourgeois who have put their pens at the service of the working class and who have become Communists without ceasing to live as petits bourgeois? But no, that's misconstruing them. These intellectuals have what we lack: the class reflex. It can be a question obviously only of a conditioned reflex, since they have rarely come out of the proletariat and since things are fixed so that they never see it. But each time they learn that an innocent Communist, like Rajk, has been hanged, or that a workers' crowd has been fired on as in eastern Berlin, as in Poznan, as in Budapest, this news brings on in them an abundant secretion from their salivary glands accompanied by the repeated cry of "Class struggle! Unity!"

In *L'Humanité* of November 30, I read under the by-line of Laurent Casanova remarks which seem more pertinent at first and which sink suddenly into paranoia: "Every analysis of the events which neglects or challenges the existence and the activity, in the Peoples Democracies, of social forces hostile to revolutionary transformations, organized and supported by world imperialism which uses them for goals of internal subversion and for its goals of war against the socialist camp is an incomplete analysis."

I'm with him and I approve when he speaks of "social forces hostile to revolutionary transformations." And then I give up, suddenly discouraged, when he speaks of "the organization of forces by world imperialism." In the first place, I don't know what "world imperialism" is: inside the Western bloc there are imperialisms which most often oppose each other, witness the

"Suez affair." If one wants to say, "American imperialism," then say it, it will be clearer. But this thinking no longer knows how to manipulate anything but symbols, it is as far from the truth as the Hungarian C.P. was from the masses. Any historian would try in a similar case to determine what these counterrevolutionary forces were, what strength they had at their disposal, and who had organized them. All that Mr. Casanova leaves in the dark. Of these forces, I will speak later. As to their organization, what does he know? Only what we know: there's the Kerstein amendment and his "billions of refugees," there are the appeals from Radio Free Europe, there is the National Committee for Free Europe. These are instruments of propaganda; their origins are very diverse, also their goals and their financing. There exists in Munich a radio station, financed by the State Department, which speaks to the Russian people. But Radio Free Europe, as far as I can judge from the information at my disposal, is supported by the refugees themselves;[1] and the programs are so diverse that the Polish station was heard begging Poland to "remain calm," on these same October days when the Hungarian station was inciting Budapest to revolt. As for the Emergency Committee to Send Arms to Hungary, it would be cited pointlessly: it was constituted *after* the uprising. All right, in any case this propaganda is inexcusable, its effects have been disastrous. But it's only propaganda. Are you unaware that "American imperialism" has always hesitated between two policies: that of "containment" and that of "roll-back"? That these two policies correspond to groups with divergent compositions and interests? That "containment" has always won out *in fact*? That this uncertainty in American policy, sometimes encour-

---

[1] I realize that one could ask *from where* these refugees draw their means of existence. But in all fairness it's after investigation, and not before, that it must be decided.

aging, sometimes abandoning the refugees, has as a consequence a very real paralysis of their services? That the refugees themselves are sapped by internal conflicts, by frequently merciless struggles. Why, if you know all that, do you represent world imperialism as a firm and indivisible force which goes straight to its goal and achieves the impossible? For after all, I know counterrevolutionary propaganda and I freely admit that it is accompanied by espionage. But you will not make me believe that one could *right in the midst of the Rakosi terror* organize and arm commandos on Hungarian territory; where did the arms come from? Were they parachuted in? It was possible in France, under the occupation, because the entire country was helping the resistance. But in a country as divided as Hungary, it's entirely unlikely. What? In twelve years, Rakosi never heard mention of the secret militia? When he had the Rajk trial, he didn't take the opportunity to denounce the supplies parachuted in?[1] And who was teaching

---

[1] A Communist challenger is willing to make me one concession: "Rakosi, instead of hanging innocent people, would have done better to outwit the counterrevolutionaries." But that's slandering Rakosi: he found the time to do both. Never in Hungary did they cease—even under Nagy's Government—exhorting the Hungarians to vigilance nor keeping watch on the former officers of the Horthy Army nor seeking out caches of arms. The text of a Hungarian writer will be read further on [This text is not in *Situations Vol. VII*, but can be found in *Les Temps Modernes*. TR.] which clearly shows that denunciations were not infrequent and that the Government took them very seriously: a former officer, seventy-six years old, was arrested if his neighbors accused him of possessing a gun. I don't presume to criticize these defensive measures: I'm simply saying that they made the parachuting and stocking of arms practically impossible. The reciprocal distrust, the conflict of interests and the old hatreds, the encouragements given to informing, everything incited the peasants to keep a sharp eye on each other. No doubt that they were discontent with the regime and with collectivization: but they were struggling in their way by passive resistance; they would not have tolerated in their villages or fields the presence of armed groups whose discovery would have perhaps brought on a massacre. It mustn't be forgotten either that the Hungarian great plain is ill-suited to the movements of guerrillas and snipers. Today, the fights take place in the marshes or in the narrow mountainous region which serves as a refuge for the insurgents.

the counterrevolutionaries to handle modern arms? Where did they drill? In the countryside? But it's in Budapest that the disorders broke out. The commandos had already proceeded there? We'll come back to this hypothesis later on. I will recall only a few facts: when the Avos, on the approaches to the Parliament, started to fire on the crowd, *it was unarmed* and so numerous that the first rows, caught by the press of the others, had to take the fire without being able to flee or defend themselves. It's at this moment that some students went to beg the Hungarian soldiers in their barracks to come to their aid. The latter were still hesitating; they joined the insurgents later: but, after a moment, the gates of a barrack opened and four trucks loaded with arms took off in the direction of Parliament. Where then was the American hardware? And where was the organization? The French C.P., misled by the "cold war," sees everything in military terms: if reactionaries take part in a riot, it immediately sees them helmeted, with flame throwers and bazookas. When will it understand that these interpretations don't belong to Marxism but to mythology? When will it understand that it is necessary to gather the facts before explaining them, that Marxist method allows figuring out experience but not suppressing it.

Not right away, that's certain. The continuation of the paragraph in Casanova's article, more theoretical, filled me with amazement and made me despair of official Marxism. It begins well enough: "Two essential factors must be taken into account: the faults of the parties and the counterrevolutionary activity, and must be united in an analysis which is in the perspective of the class struggle." Nothing better. But wait a bit: "The procedure of thought which would consist in seeing only one side of the question or in establishing between these factors an hierarchical order is a hazardous procedure which can falsify the whole analysis." No hierarchical order? What does that mean? We are evaluating the conditions of an historical fact and, what's more, we are intending to *bring them together in the analysis*. Must we renounce determining their respective importance? In mechanics, each force acts as if it were alone; but in a historical perspective, it is necessary to envisage the reciprocal action of the factors, to study the modifications which each of them produces on the others. Is this possible without taking note at every moment of the polarizations, of the regroupings, of a perpetual play of dominant and recessive forces, in short a shifting hierarchy of conditionings? When Marxism says of a rising class that it is a matter of history, isn't it establishing a hierarchy? When *L'Humanité* congratulates the Red Army for having prevented world war, isn't it establishing a hierarchy? What can this lead to, this strange decision to adopt two different and equally incomplete explanations and to develop them along parallel lines while claiming to unite them, without ever comparing them or bringing them into contact? To the negation pure and simple of all dialectic. For real forces are substituted the isolated concepts of the mind; two abstractions are present at once—the "faults" of the Government and the forces organized by world imperialism—for the sole purpose of balancing the first by the second and of ending up with the classical schema: right-wing opportunism will exaggerate the importance of the faults, left-wing sectarianism will put everything on the account of imperialism.

Marx would have laughed at these pompous asses who take the class struggle for a Platonic Idea or who bring it in like a *Deus ex machina*. Even knowledge of prior facts and of the structures of the new society—knowledge which moreover is totally lacking to Messrs. Casanova and Fajon—can only imperfectly illuminate a process which has its own history and in the course of which the relationships have not ceased to evolve. What it would be necessary to show are the real contradictions of the Hungarian insurrection and the shifting relationships which are established among the classes. Let us try:

The clearest fact is that, up to October 23, the demands bore essentially on democratization. Nationalism remained in the background: the Rakosists[1] had extolled it in words and humiliated it by all their acts. This treatment had strengthened it in people's hearts. But it feared, perhaps, to show itself in all its nudity: it would have appeared then as a terrible negative power; the hatred of the occupying power would have taken it over. Fortunately, social demands allowed it to express itself without revealing itself; it was the core of and the primary condition for democratic reforms: Could Hungary seek its own way towards socialism without having been given first of all its complete sovereignty? The most concrete and most immediate claims promptly fused with the national requirement: How to raise the standard of living without making a new distribution of investments, that is to say without establishing production plans with the collaboration of Hungarian experts only? How to give back to the unions their true functions if norms were fixed arbitrarily and in terms of Russian demands? It seemed then that communism in Hungary could not be saved without entirely reconsidering the relations of the Hungarians and Russians.

It is on this social ground that without distinction all those who were calling for democratization took their stand. This

---

[1] It wasn't entirely by chance that Rakosi had suppressed the national holiday. (Let's imagine Maurice Thorez in power and decreeing that the 14th of July will not be celebrated.) And if he demolished an old church of Budapest, a place of annual pilgrimage, to erect alongside of its site a monstrous statue of Stalin, this wasn't inadvertent either.

unity concealed divergences of interests and perspectives: for the Communist opposition, it was a question above all of finding contact with the masses again: sovereignty, however desirable it might be, seemed the principal means to give new value to and to carry forward the experiment; for the conservative petite bourgeoisie,[1] on the contrary, the means was democratization, the end was national independence. Then again, the members of the C.P. were hoping to loosen the Rakosi vise, revive the Party, come back "to Leninism," but they were not envisaging for an instant modifying the system of the Single Party. On the other hand the Social-Democrats and the Small Property Owners[2] conceived of democracy only as a return to a plurality of parties.[3] These divergences did not stop

---

[1] Numerous, I realize, even among the workers. Rakosi, in fact, had systematically "proletarized" it.

[2] Often called the "Smallholders Party" and is so listed in the Glossary.

[3] After the trial of the right-wing Social-Democrats (November, 1947) and the purging of the Social-Democratic Party (March, 1948), social-democracy and the C.P. had held a Congress of unification, June 13, 1948. From this had come the Party of Socialist Workers in which the *now purged* social-democratic Left had been purely and simply absorbed by the Party. I will call this entity, hereafter, the "Hungarian Communist Party" for more clarity. The Social-Democrats to whom I allude above are electors and sympathizers who maintained a social-democratic orientation without being *represented* by an autonomous group. Curiously enough, moreover, after trials, purges and fusion, the headquarters of the Social-Democratic Party still existed in Budapest, a pure, empty organism without contact with real currents. The Small Property Owners Party had not been dissolved either but absorbed into formations of the "United Front" type. The Hungarian Presidium (that is to say, *the* presidents of the Republic) is today still presided over by a former Small Property Owner: Dobi, who has no other function than to represent in his person the diversity of the parties. But in the countryside and in the petite bourgeoisie of the towns, this Small Property Owner current has never diminished in intensity. The *paper structures (formations de façade)*, totally under the tutelage of the C.P., and the *real political currents* no longer had anything in common. A noncommunist party could be officially *designated* but it no longer existed outside of its name: its reality continued to exist in the people because it represented certain interests, certain classes (we'll come back to this), but it had lost its name and its power of expression. The enormous error of the C.P. is that it thought to "play the game" by keeping a few

there: of the former noncommunist formations, some, certain that the C.P. would be opposed to any election, had contented themselves with an actual participation in the Government; others were holding back to demand in due course the return to a parliamentary system. The latter were to divide a little later on a question, the urgency of which wasn't yet apparent: Was it necessary to reconstitute only the parties which were governing in 1945 or should one tolerate the resurrection of older factions and the birth of new formations? In the first case, one was arbitrarily restricting the *liberal* principle; in the second, under the pretense of total liberalization, one risked opening the door to fascism. But in the universal confusion of the first two weeks of October, these attitudes were neither clear nor settled; they were able to coexist or to follow each other within the same group or the same individual. What they all had in common was the rejection of the Rakosi dictatorship and, deep down, the national claim.

In the Writers Union, in the Petöfi Circle, the movement of the intellectuals had been above all *critical* and *negative*: it had entrenched itself in a more and more violent opposition, instead of building up positive projects for government. It's because the situation required *this attitude* and none other, the function of the intellectuals was to represent negativity: it was not a matter of suggesting to Rakosi that he make certain improvements in the system; it was necessary to reveal his crimes to everyone, to discredit him completely, to force him to resign. It is known that they succeeded. If their criticism

---

political personalities who were outsiders to communism, by giving them high offices and by presenting them, "enframed," in prefabricated elections instead of evaluating the situation and of defining its own action in terms of the real circumstances: it would have understood that the depth of the noncommunist currents made it incumbent on it to act *on the masses* and that meant establishing a *real* alliance with the democratic parties and combatting their influence by the effects of a positive policy.

had an undeniable influence on the working masses, it was precisely because it was negative. The events in Poland showed the course to follow: one must unite and bring to power, before all other changes, national Communists who were able to negotiate with the U.S.S.R. The entire country was demanding Nagy. This Communist had a great role to play: the program, the methods, the rate, the extent of the democratization, nothing had been defined; for the moment, democratization was the object of powerful and specific demands, but demands which obviously had to be ordered in the perspective of practical possibilities. The writer who was denouncing Zhdanovism and the worker who was demanding a raise in his real wage both contributed to determining the direction and the content of democratization. It was further necessary to elaborate, on the basis of these givens, a total policy which took into account at the same time Russian inclinations, Hungarian aspirations, the economic situation and counterrevolutionary threats. This is what constituted Mr. Nagy's chance: for the Hungarians, democratization had to merge, at least in the beginning, with the action of a sincere government which would be politically experienced, which would rely on experts and technicians and which would be competent enough to envisage the problem in its entirety. By taking the head of the reformist movement, by speaking all the truth, by *surpassing* certain demands, by explaining immediately to the country why other demands could not be immediately satisfied, the Nagy Government could increase the influence of the C.P. and diminish that of the Social-Democrats; a sincere and total *democratization* made *liberalization* impossible.

On the night of the 23rd everything is in the balance; democratization becomes a secondary consideration, the Soviet aggression provokes an explosion of nationalism. All these men, just the day before, were trying to reach agreement on a political and social program: they join together within a United Front, spontaneously constituted, whose immediate task is to fight the aggressor. The Russian intervention has tightened their bonds, it has crystallized their latent anti-Sovietism, it has stirred up this easily excitable population, it has given it other goals, essentially negative. One should not see in this revolt either a blind and disorderly reaction or a movement organized in a single direction. Let Mr. Garaudy reassure himself: it is not a question of spontaneity. Years of oppression have moulded these men and the real bonds which unite them. The unity of the Party, of its methods and of its terror has given rise in the people—in spite of the divergences of interests—to the diffuse unity of refusal. It was a question of identical reactions, unorganized but not isolated; no one needed to speak to know that his personal attitude was that of all. With us, exploitation relies on disintegrating forces: a constant effort is necessary to maintain unity. The Rakosi dictatorship, in contrast, in seeking to achieve integration by violence, brought the workers together but it brought them together *against it;* in uniting them by phoney ties which masked their dependence, it made them become aware of their true relationships. This relationship remained halfway between real unity, which presupposes the organization of a diversity, and identity, the simple coexistence of like particles which are unaware of each other: it was, if you wish, the deep but unconscious awareness of a negative identity. That's what explains the original character of the insurrection: it is sporadic, chaotic; no underground force, no clandestine leadership prepared it. But this apparent disorder covers a nascent order: each group of combatants is conscious of representing all the people, precisely because its particular reaction is a particularization of the general reaction. It doesn't need, in order to perceive it, to know the episodes of the battle in detail: for each insurgent, these fights are already *national*, they contain the promise and show the necessity of insurrectional unity. Each group provides itself with leaders; after a little while, contacts are established between the leaders: some of them acquire a considerable influence (the most influential is Maleter, a Communist). But the insurrection will remain to the end a many-headed hydra. And it is true that an adventurer, attracted by fascism, occupies with his men—of whom some were Communists—the *Szabad Nep* building. But he withdraws shortly afterwards without having molested the newspapermen and, two or three days later, at the first conference of the insurrectional units, the leaders present unanimously, less one vote, break all ties with him.

The Communist newspapers have often mentioned the presence of armed émigrés but they haven't given any proof of it. They speak vaguely of American arms but half-heartedly. And among the prisoners? Not the least agent from abroad. In Berlin, Germans who had come from the West had been caught: their photos were published, their trials set in motion. Nothing of the sort in Hungary: how convenient it would be, however! But after all, on the 23rd, the Red Army was occupying the city and cutting it off from the rest of the world; it leaves it on the 30th and that to encircle it. The presence of Soviet troops certainly doesn't prevent infiltration, but it makes unlikely the massive arrival of fascist reinforcements. Peter Frey, the Communist correspondent for the *Daily Worker*, makes quite a bit of the information given by Austrian Communists according to which, before the 4th of November, 2,000 émigrés armed and trained by the Americans are supposed to have entered Hungary. Were these Communists well-informed? By what witnesses? One doesn't know. And if I report the fact, it is out of consideration for the personage of Frey, who has written, as is known, articles rejected for excess of good faith. In any case, it's the only piece of information worthy of examination which we possess. And, even if one really wishes to hold on to it, one will observe that 2,000 émigrés, even armed, are incapable of changing by themselves the course of a revolution. Besides, since we are dealing with unverifiable news reports, I must point out that, according to the correspondent of the *New Statesman*, whose reputation for honesty is established, up to November 4, the frontier stations which were in the hands of the insurgents were turning back all the émigrés who were trying to return to Hungary, in particular Ferenc Nagy, the head of the emigration. It was said that there had been *commandos*. Communist observers have confirmed to me that it was being said in Budapest. It was being said because people had heard it said. But these same observers covered the city in all directions, from October 24 to November 3, without ever meeting any of them nor meeting anyone who had managed to see them at work. Let's remember those "bandits" who were seen everywhere at the time of our Revolution and who weren't anywhere. For many Hungarians—particularly on the Left—the memory of 1919 and of the White terror had not been erased. They thought they were reliving their past. And even if these commandos did exist, were they putting Democracy in danger? Let us think rather of the others, the immense majority of insurgents, workers, students, soldiers, petits bourgeois: no one dares any more today to call them fascists, *even* Mr. Waldeck-Rochet. Mr. Stil notes with disdain the extreme youth of the combatants (zazous of sorts): this scorn marvelously suits the representative of a sclerotic apparatus which no longer even succeeds in recruiting among the young and whose average age rises from year to year. But his remark backfires: in 1945, in this Hungary divided, devas-

35

tated, prostrated by years of fascism, on whom then could the regime count if not on the youth which it was going to mould? It had twelve years to bind them to it and the only result of its efforts is that the young people are the most eager to overthrow it. How pedantic and scholastic their teachers must have been! How simplistic and stupid the teaching of Marxism must have been! Among the students there are those whom Stalin turned from Marx: these students, deprived of all contact with Western culture, have no substitute ideology; they turn towards their national literature which was always political and which had reflected for more than a hundred years the people's aspiration to independence. No doubt that they are nationalists and *only* nationalists; some remained *on the Left* but their hatred of bureaucratic despotism extends to the principles to which their tyrants appeal: they want above all *freedoms*, freedom of speech, of expression, of criticism, of information, of assembly. These entirely legitimate claims, they unfortunately do not believe can be based on a Marxism of which they have been shown only the authoritarian aspect; hence these claims produce in them, as in certain writers, an unconscious return to a kind of anarchism.[1] No doubt that this tendency can be dangerous, but in the long run: it led to lack of discipline much

---

[1] In reading the Hungarian texts which *Les Temps Modernes* publishes, I think that one will be struck as I was by their theoretical indecision. This Left is in crisis, it needs to re-think itself, to come back to fundamental questions, to socialist methods: but after all, isn't this what it is saying itself? The irresolution of thought marks only the impossibility of finding a substitute ideology: it would not have taken long for the undecided to come back to Marxism. To the real thing. One will profitably compare the Hungarian texts with the Polish texts which we will publish in the next issue. The caution kept up even in the midst of violence by the former Government of Poland, its curious will not to overstep the limits when already all limits had been passed, its moderation in the midst of horror and above all a rapid but progressive evolution from Poznan on permitted the new leaders to effect reform while remaining Marxists and Communists.

more than to fascism; and this lack of discipline, as long as the fights lasted, gave way before the voluntary discipline of the fighters. And then there were the others—the better, perhaps—those for whom the cramped catechism of the Stalinists had not been able to hide the immense possibilities of Marxism. These latter were fighting to save the culture.

Under the name of Rakosism, it is socialism that many petits bourgeois are consciously or unconsciously fighting. But they are not very numerous among the insurgents and then it would be a serious error (Mr. Casanova, I'm sure, will not make it) to confuse them with the members of the apparatus, the cadres, who were living in a bourgeois style and some of whom, however, took up arms. And above all, the undeniable truth is that workers formed the majority of the combatants. According to the declarations of a Hungarian unionist whom the leaders of the C.G.T. met in Prague, it seems that the workers of the industrial outskirts of the city were not armed at first. This is understandable: the insurrection broke out in the center of Budapest. I have said that the first deliveries of arms were made hastily by the barracks to the crowd: there was a bit of everything in this crowd, workers, but also and above all, students and petits bourgeois. These first handouts quickly exhausted the most accessible stocks and, for several hours or several days, the personnel of the large factories had to remain empty handed. But it has been proven today that Nagy undertook systematically to arm the proletariat—probably through the intermediary of the unions—in order to set authentically revolutionary forces against an eventual return of reaction. One will not contest, undoubtedly, the testimony of Marshal Zhukov who, on October 30, said: "I consider that the fact of giving arms to the workers proves that the new Hungarian Government effectively relies on the working class."

Unfortunately for him, the working class used these arms to defend the Hungarian people against the Soviet soldiers: it's at Csepel, *among the workers*, that the battle raged; it's there that it lasted the longest. What would one think, here, of an insurrection which would develop primarily in the "Red Belt" of Paris? Would one dare to call it fascist? It's here that they give us the spontaneity bit: You know very well, says Mr. Garaudy, that one cannot abandon the proletariat to its spontaneous reactions. That's quite correct if one means by it that the workers' movement must determine itself daily through a tight dialectic which opposes the cadres and the masses the better to unite them; that the former, through education, sincere explanations and agitation, must struggle against the dangers from the outside; that the latter, as soon as they are set in motion, go beyond their leaders and pull them along by radicalizing the demands themselves. But this no longer means anything if one is trying to say that a socialist government has the right to repress by force the insurrection of a proleteriat which it reduced to despair. For, after all, if we abandon myths and symbols, what was Lenin trying to say when he spoke of spontaneity? This, very simply: that different factors —among which we can mention the very condition of the worker, the fear of a bloody repression, the ideological propaganda of the bourgeoisie, the forces of massification—*in a capitalist country* lead the worker who is politically uneducated to place his hope in reformism.[1] What sense does the theory maintain when its application is attempted to the armed revolution of a proletariat in a socialist country? Marx explains that the revolutionary strength of the worker in bourgeois societies "is born from the contradiction between his

---

[1] It is not a matter then, for Lenin, of bringing into question the value of this workers' spontaneity but rather of proving that spontaneity does not exist. Except, we might say, after unification, in and through the distancing of the leaders.

human *nature* and his real life existence which is the manifest, decisive and total negation of this nature." Despite the socialist form of Hungarian society, no one dreams of denying that this contradiction still existed there; besides one will find the proof of it in the testimonies which follow this article. Where does spontaneity come in here? It should, in a socialist country, predispose the proletariat *all the more* to reformism.[1]

It is not spontaneity then that pushes the masses to armed insurrection, *it is need.* I am very much afraid that they seek to cover with the name of spontaneity one of the major contradictions which gave birth to the Stalinist system: the contradiction of need and plan. We will come back to it. Certainly the composition of the Hungarian proletariat is far from being homogeneous: out of 1,600,000 workers, slightly more than a third were drawn in by the superindustrialization of the 1950s. To measure the incredible rapidity of this population unheaval, let us recall that Budapest went *in six years*—1948–1954—from 1,058,288 inhabitants to 1,700,000. These newcomers, disconcerted by the brutality of methods, by the rapidity of changes,[2] surely kept, to one degree or another, their peasant mentality. Perhaps some of them, left to their

---

[1] What one would call "spontaneity," in this perspective, would be rather the mutism, the apparent inertia of the Hungarian proletariat around 1955; one will find the description and interpretation of it in the texts of Laszlo Pal, Stakhanovite milling machine operator; Bela Kiss, smith; Ervin Eisner, milling machine operator, which we are publishing in this issue. [See note p. 25. TR.] This passivity—which masks a profound revolt—is the attitude which an abandoned proletariat adopts *provisionally.* "Finally someone is bothering about us," says one worker a propos of a newspaper article. Another: "Let the leaders come to us." A third: "Some leaders came but they only invited about fifty workers," etc. A Hungarian reporter adds: "They have a craving for humanity."

[2] Brutal increase of norms, sudden "nationalization" of a factory or of an entire sector of production, appearance of new machines to which the worker doesn't have time to adapt himself, reduced workload during the first twenty days of the month (because the raw materials aren't delivered in time, etc.), followed by a crushing overload during the last ten days, etc.

"spontaneity," that is to say to their small town routines, would have let themselves be tempted by political adventure: but they were solidly surrounded by older workers, who had known the Horthy dictatorship and who had true revolutionary traditions to call on. These experienced combatants were joined by young people who came to industry immediately after the war, between 1945 and 1948; at this time the rural exodus was slower, the work norms lower, the transformations less brusque: they were integrated into the working class without difficulty. It is true that the most combative nucleus of the proletariat, before 1939, was social-democratic and the C.P. practically didn't exist. But let's not start thinking of our Guy Mollets: the Party, contrary to ours, represented the proletariat and not the petite bourgeoisie; it is a matter of *hardened* socialists moulded by a dangerous and arduous struggle against a dictatorial government. In spite of its official disappearance, the influence of social-democracy persisted and the criminal imbecility of the Rakosi regime reinforced it. Despite the bureaucratic tyranny, the scarcity of unskilled labor (a result of the accelerated industrialization) neutralized the bureaucratic dictatorship: poorly nourished, poorly housed, overworked, spied upon, the workers, in spite of their mutism, knew their weight, they became aware of their true importance. Overwhelmed by the degrading lies of the propaganda, by police inquisition, they sensed their stock going up because of the extreme need for them. Thus the contradictions of the regime were fortifying their courage and their class feeling. They took up arms to overthrow a tyranny which was leading the country to ruin, but never—were they Communists or Social-Democrats—did they question the socialization of industry. For a long time they had accepted sacrificing themselves to the socialist Hungary; they revolted when they saw that these useless sacrifices were not preventing either the decay of the nation or the liquidation—near or remote—of the socialist bases.

Whatever one may think of the Budapest uprising and of what would have resulted from it without the November 4 intervention, one could not insist too much on the essential fact which characterizes it: the workers were in arms, they did not want—what folly would have pushed them to it?—to hand back the factories to the capitalists but, as the outcome proved, to assure themselves the control of industry by electing factory committees and workers' councils. These workers' councils which were constituted as early as the first days of the insurrection, which never ceased to function, and which still function, it is they which transformed the armed resistance into a general strike; it is they which succeeded, in several provincial cities, in dealing with reactionary disturbances; it is they which forced Kadar to negotiate with them: after the crushing of the revolt, they are the only live force, both socialist and nationalist, which opposes the Russians and the reconstitution of the bureaucracy. Who then would dare to deny that they represent a positive past for Hungarian socialism? In particular, I would like to ask the Communists who still hesitate, if this strike prolonged in spite of terror and massive arrests, if these negotiations continuously broken off and continuously resumed, about which Radio-Budapest daily informs us, are not of a nature to cast a serious doubt on the counterrevolutionary character of the Hungarian resistance? The Soviet newspapers claim that the Red Army intervened against the insurgents, alongside the workers. The workers throw a humiliating denial at them: their strike and the maintenance of their demands prove that they were and they remain *with* the insurgents and against the Red Army. This smashed revolution, whatever its risks and faults have been, the Hungarian working class takes on and becomes its heir and guardian. Who then, when the Russians themselves are forced to admit the Budapest negotiations, who, among the leaders of the French Communist party, will dare to challenge the testimony of an entire proletariat?[1]

However, from October 23 to November 1, the shift toward the Right is undeniable; the situation deteriorates. Again it is necessary to be specific: this change did not have for its cause the sudden apparition of fascist demons surging up from somewhere or other; it is a series of disequilibriums within the insurrectional movement, a kind of internal metabolism which tends to modify the structure of the groups and the relationship of forces among the combatants.

The principal reason for this evolution must be sought in the conditions of the first Russian intervention. The Hungarian bureaucracy had long since lost its credit with the masses; the Communist Party was suspect. But, in spite of eight years of tyranny, of monstrous or grotesque errors, of crimes, the chances for a national and democratic communism remained intact. The masses are realists: at the beginning of a strike movement or revolution, they demand the *minimum*, an almost imperceptible improvement of their condition. It would have seemed inopportune and ridiculous, even to the Social-Democratic workers, to call for the liquidation of the C.P. It

---

[1] When I was writing these words, Kadar had not yet dared to dissolve the workers' councils. Now, it's done. Therefore, I change my question and ask: "What is this socialism which is bent on destroying the instruments of control elected by the proletariat? And if it recognized them yesterday as the true representatives of the people, how can it, without disqualifying itself, have their leaders arrested today? And if Zhukov congratulated the Nagy Government for basing itself on the working class, shouldn't he condemn a government which wants to gag it? My Communist friends have sometimes cried out: "The Soviets everywhere!" It's a fine program. Henceforth it will be necessary to make it a bit more precise: "The Soviets everywhere except in Hungary."

was well-known that the Soviets would have confidence only in a Communist government and that a Communist government alone would be able to negotiate with them. On the 23rd, some hours before the insurrection, all of the population of Budapest was in the streets; but one forgets too often that the initial demonstration had taken place in honor of Poland: the events of Warsaw, the Polish victory of October 18 had profoundly moved the Hungarians; perhaps certain of them were honoring Gomulka *in spite of* his belonging to the C.P., but whether they wished it or not, their homages were being addressed to a Communist. This immense celebration is proof that the masses were asking for a Hungarian "Gomulkism": nothing more, nothing less. Besides, social-democracy was practically disarmed: it was, for the workers, a fighting tradition, a way of life. An unorganized opposition, social-democracy had profited for some years from the popular discontent, but its boundaries were shifting, many workers were Communists and Social-Democrats at the same time. And then, above all, it was incapable of presenting a constructive program: Marxist; it was in agreement with the C.P. to defend the bases of socialism and in agreement with the Communist opposition to call for democratization. If Nagy, called back October 15—and perhaps even the 23rd—had taken immediate measures to raise the standard of living, to stabilize the norms, and to endow the workers with truly defensive mechanisms, if he had declared his desire to reorganize the national economy, if he, like Gomulka, had unreservedly revealed the extent of the disasters and given the general lines of a plan for reconstruction, if he had announced finally that he was immediately initiating negotiations with the Soviets, he would have struck a terrible blow at the Social-Democratic opposition by taking away its very reason for existence. In a word,

43

all could have been saved, and first of all the Communist Party itself.

But it was Gerö who was ruling. By calling for the intervention of the Russians, more from the stubbornness of a fool than from cowardice, he disqualified the C.P. at one stroke; the first machine gun burst made it irremediably the foreigner's Party. That was false: a large number of militants, mixed in with the crowd, unreservedly approved of the demonstrators; Hungarian Communists fell from the bullets of Russian Communists; this criminal folly was only the shudder of a dying Stalinism. But everything transpired for the crowd—and, the next day, for the entire country—as if the C.P. had revealed its true face; the insurgents refused to see in it anything but the ferocious instrument of Soviet oppression. For the moment, nationalism was welded to anti-Sovietism and anticommunism. The Communist opposition, however, rallied the insurrection; its members were warmly welcomed, some of them won influence over their comrades: but they were listened to *by virtue of* being insurgents and *in spite of* their belonging to the C.P. Nagy himself was in disrepute: he had been called on when everything was lost and he had committed the error of accepting power without posing conditions. Above all, the responsibility for calling in the Soviets had been attributed to him first of all. He denied it. And, anyway, it is true that he didn't issue an appeal *qua* head of the Hungarian government. But the insurgents said Gerö had his criminal decision approved by the Central Committee and he received a unanimity of votes: now, Nagy was present. To which his few partisans answered: He was attending the session of the Central Committee because it had been convoked, but he was not yet a member of it, and it is much later that the election actually took place. Perhaps they wanted to compromise him:

in this case, the maneuver succeeded. It is necessary to add that he was, in the beginning, virtually a prisoner of the Central Committee where the Rakosists were in the majority: this is what explains that he did at first[1]—feebly—disapprove of the insurrection instead of taking its leadership and giving it a program which would have permitted channelizing it. This ambiguous attitude made him lose his popularity briefly; when he freed himself, it was too late: this Government called for too long, sullied by a massacre of which it was innocent, was displeasing the Soviets without pleasing the insurgents. The former reproached it for ceding to popular pressure; the latter with promising what it would not be allowed to carry out. One sees the contradiction: a Communist government was necessary to undertake democratization with the consent of the Russians and to push it to the end without abandoning the principles of Marxism; the only government possible was, therefore, that of Nagy; but, as early as the night of the 23rd, Gerö had undermined his authority. The provisional disqualification of Nagy was confronting the insurgents with an unexpected fact: a power vacuum. At the same time, Soviet shells were blowing up Marxism and this brutal liquidation of the dominant ideology left the insurrection without a program and without resource. United in the national struggle, they had not yet found a common denominator for their demands; no political judgment came along to illuminate their struggle; the insurrection was *going on* without *knowing itself*. In the western part of the country, it seemed that the reactionary forces must triumph; everywhere else the majority wanted to protect the social achievements. But the ideological uncertainty risked at every moment breaking up the insurgents'

---

[1] On October 24 and the days following, he was promising immunity to the insurgents who would lay down their arms.

front and throwing them against each other. In some quarters in Budapest, armed workers were preparing to fight at the same time against the Soviets, against the Avos, and against the armed groups who would want to call the nationalizations into question. The relations of the unions—organs of the Rakosist dictatorship—and the workers' councils were not defined either. In the unions themselves, the adversaries of the system were beginning to fight the bureaucratic majority. The unionist of whom I spoke earlier summed this up in a single phrase: "Everyone was against everyone." This situation could not last. The differences had to be overcome at any price. This is what transformed for some the desire for *democratization* into the urgent demand for *liberalization*. The only ones who could, in fact, substitute themselves for the Communists, were the Social-Democrats; but they had first to be recognized as a party. And how to urge *for them* the reconstitution of parties without asking for it, at the same time, for all the dissolved organizations whose former members were fighting at their side, in particular for the Small Property Owners Party. But, with this Party, whose very name is a program, agricultural socialization which the peasants, besides, had already undertaken to liquidate, was done for. And how to prevent the appearance or the reappearance of other political forces? The Catholics, who already had freed Cardinal Mindszenty, could they be forbidden to form a group? In the name of what, since, in this extreme confusion where Marxists were struggling against Marxists, were the principles of Marxism abandoned? And the ex-shopkeepers, the still numerous artisans, who had never rallied to the regime? One could indeed consider them class enemies: that didn't prevent them from paying with their blood for the right to express their opinion. The class struggle gives way—as it often happens in

wars of liberation—to the fight against the foreigner. From the
moment when he takes up arms, every Hungarian tacitly receives from the other insurgents the right to command respect
for his point of view, in the immediate present and later, after
victory. And these men of divergent, sometimes even opposing
interests will not remain united in the battle unless they are
agreed on calling for an election: only elections can initiate
and guarantee peaceful competition among their representatives.

Rakosism was neither a fascist dictatorship nor a run-of-the-
mill tyranny: it represented socialization after all; only it represented it poorly, which is worse than not representing it at
all. The suicide of this monster was to leave an irreparable
void. By violence, by terror, it had integrated all classes into
the regime: the insurrection was necessarily to present itself as
a disintegration. Forces which had been hidden or restrained
for a long time necessarily were to reappear: deprived of an
arbiter by the break up of the C.P., the insurgents shifted towards the Right in order to maintain the unity of their fight.
The immediate requirements of the struggle forced them to demand a return to the parliamentary regime. On the morning
of October 30, the situation is thoroughly paradoxical: there
is a government still. But the U.S.S.R., already, is refusing it
its confidence. As for the insurgents, they consider it an abstract force whose only function is to validate their demands.
Under their pressure, Nagy continuously alters his Cabinet so
it will reflect the insurrectional groups; but, by the same token,
he loses all raison d'être, for he is not really either the adversary of the insurgents nor their incarnation. Thus, always
snowed under, always an hour or a day behind, this Government is outdistanced, the insurrection has it in tow. With each
new concession, the Soviet leaders feel their distrust being re-

inforced: they consider Nagy to be a traitor. In fact, he is a sincere Communist whom the course of events is in process of *de-Communizing*. A Communist chief, indeed, relies on a structured Party, which, in theory at least, assures links with the masses. But the Party has gone up in smoke. The Central Committee is hiding, the militants are on the firing line in the midst of the insurgents. When they negotiate with Nagy, the representatives of the insurrectional groups never address themselves to the Communist, but to the nationalist head of a transitional government. That's the whole tough luck of this good and sincere man: subjectively, he remains faithful to his Party; objectively, everything happens as if he had resigned from it. The masses, after having insisted on freedom within the regime, now demand freedom of choosing the regime which pleases them.

Thus, it is accurate that the insurrection was going to the Right; that doesn't mean that elements of the Right were getting the upper hand, but that the struggle against the foreigner was of itself creating conditions which would permit them to take power one day. Free elections—irreproachable in principle—could bring back a majority of Small Property Owners in the new Parliament.[1]

It is likewise the suicide of the C.P. which changed the nature of the national exigency. Certainly, the insurgents' fight against the Soviet troops could only have one significance: they

---

[1]In Hungary there exists a kind of population equilibrium between the primary sector, on the one hand, and the secondary and tertiary sectors, on the other. But the Party of Small Property Owners got fifty-three percent of the votes in 1945; it had then picked up a certain number of votes in the urban centers. Tomorrow it can become the party of the rural inhabitants and that of the city petite bourgeoisie. The C.P. can count henceforth—at the maximum—on only four or five percent of the votes. Even assuming that all the other votes turn to social democracy, the socialist Left runs a strong risk of being in the minority.

were calling for the departure of the Red Army; this departure itself was to inaugurate a new phase in the relations between Hungary and the U.S.S.R. But *neutralization* is only a very particular form of the return to sovereignty. There are others more positive, more fruitful: for example, an alliance proclaiming at the same time the independence of the signatory countries and the community of their interests, which signifies that they will reconsider together and as equals their economic, political and military relations. When the Party was governing, many people reproached it with obeying the U.S.S.R. in a servile fashion: precisely because of that, the same Party, renovated, democratized, with fresh leaders and national ones, could serve as a real and effective intermediary between the Hungarian people and the Soviet Government. In all the Peoples Democracies, indeed, communism and nationalism are in profound contradiction; the national Communist is a man who has lived this contradiction, who has been moulded by it and who seeks to go beyond it without abandoning either of the two terms. By this token, Gomulka saved Poland without breaking with the U.S.S.R. By this token also, the disqualification and the collapse of the Hungarian C.P. was to break every concrete link between the two nations and destroy all the organisms of mediation: this Party, as a matter of fact, when it was dictatorial, headed up and directed itself, under Russian control, all of the joint enterprises—whether they were economic or cultural. The criminal folly of Gerö had the effect of closing the door to all negotiated solutions which the U.S.S.R. could accept, by suppressing the organs and the constituted bodies which enjoyed its confidence: Nagy, de-Communized in fact, didn't represent the Party either in the eyes of the Russians or in those of the insurgents. Between Hungary and Russia, there was only one relationship left:

combat; the middle road was lacking. Insurgents, Russians: that's all; the former could conceive of independence only in its most immediate form, that is to say, before everything else, as the departure of the latter. And neutralization did no more than to reflect this demand: the ties cut, what could the Hungarians call for except coexistence in its most elementary and most negative aspect, that is to say, in sum, pure and simple juxtaposition? It goes without saying that they sincerely believed they were calming the fears of the Soviet leaders by committing themselves to supporting the same relations or the same lack of relations with their Western neighbors. Neutralism, in itself, cannot be considered as a right-wing attitude, and the U.S.S.R., in other places, has shown itself to be favorable towards it. But it has been partial to it to the very extent that it weakened the enemy bloc. Neutrality in Hungary, was this not economic competition, on Hungarian soil, between the East and the West? was this not, shortly, perhaps, the victory of the U.S.A. and, who knows, the return of capitalism? At least that's what the Soviets were very sincerely afraid of.

Such was the balance sheet in the last days of October: the self-destruction of the C.P. imposed a negative program on the insurrection. And this negative program—free elections, neutralization—could, if it was accepted, bring Hungary back into the Western bloc. It is a lie to try to explain the shift towards the Right by an invasion of émigrés or by the sudden reappearance of counterrevolutionaries who were hiding out in the country. It is very precisely the opposite: if a few reactionary elements could, here and there, gain an audience, the fact is that the sudden volatilization of the C.P. made this shift inevitable, in spite of the insurgents themselves.

It is necessary to add that the departure of the Russian troops provoked, from the 31st on, a sudden decompression

—explosion of joy, hatred and violence—which pushed the crowd to lynch the Avos and, probably, a few Communists.[1] At the same time, Cardinal Mindszenty was speaking on the radio. His declarations gave the impression that he considered himself the inspirer, if not the chief of the reactionary forces.

Was the situation of socialism and democracy hopeless? That is what they would like to make us believe. But let's look a bit more closely. These lynchings, first of all, are atrocious. But they are mocking us when they try to intrigue us with them and give them a political significance. All the same it must not be forgotten that Rakosism was a police regime and that the Avos had made themselves detested by Communists quite as much as by "reactionaries."[2] But *above all* they wish to hide

---

[1] In Budapest, the lynchings of Communists seem to have been few. But in the provinces there were some serious settlings of accounts. And how much this argument has been abused! The fact is that it permits recourse to the sacred: "Never would workers, never would sincere socialists tolerate that a hand be laid in front of them on Communist comrades." *Therefore*, the lynchers are Arrow Cross, and if you say the contrary, you insult the proletariat. But—would this be because I don't have a feeling for the sacred?—the validity of the reasoning escapes me. If the Communist comrade is an official (*responsable*), if his opportunism and hardness of heart made him an accomplice of the Rakosist terror, if he humiliated, maltreated his subordinates, if he made himself odious by his self-importance and by the privileges he enjoyed, if he had innocent people arrested and deported, why would workers, why would sincere socialists defend him? Without a doubt they would prefer that he be judged: but who will judge him in this time of violence when the powers have collapsed? Certainly there are no grounds for approving these lynchings—some of which seem to have been of a quite abject cruelty. But what does it serve to pass censure on them? Have there ever been guiltless revolutions? A French Communist said to me: "Put yourself in our place: they're assassinating our comrades." It's true. But Rajk and Slansky were also comrades. Did the French Communists yell that they were being assassinated? When the supreme power crushes a militant, they immediately declare that he's a traitor. When the vengeance of the people is exercised on an official, it is the people who are criminal in their eyes. One sees that they made their choice.

[2] From a source which I believe reliable, I have this information: Between October 30 and November 4, about one hundred and forty Avos probably were massacred in Budapest.

an essential fact from us: that, the night of the 23rd, they gave the signal for the slaughter. Quite often, the Russian soldiers hesitated, sometimes they fraternized with the population. The Avos didn't hesitate; they took their time, aimed carefully and fired. That's what the crowd has not forgiven: Hungarians, they had fired on unarmed Hungarians. They had to be judged: agreed. But history offers a thousand examples of these lynchings: they are the result of a twice-fired hatred and a fear which changes into aggressiveness; it's the paralysis of powers which makes them possible. Today, people are trying to attribute the responsibility for these summary executions to Horthist commandos. Once upon a time, the Girondins tried to make people believe that the September Massacres had been organized: by Marat, some say, or by Robespierre. And others say: by Danton. Still others: by the Paris Commune. Today's historians are in agreement in considering that it was a matter of collective movement. Immobilized by mutual distrust and hatred, the Legislative Assembly and the Commune have no other responsibility than being unable to prevent it. In Budapest, Nagy was powerless; the insurgents were very reluctant, in the beginning, to set themselves against the people: they could scarcely, in their turn, begin firing on them. They had no other means than to win their confidence; but that required time. This slow but steady action bore its fruits; from the moment that the insurrectional committees had taken the thing in hand, the number of lynchings declined. On Saturday, the 3rd—the day before the Soviet aggression—all had returned to order. As for Cardinal Mindszenty, the Stalinist press makes him its bogeyman. But it is not enough to reproduce the words of an old man, worn-out from suffering and set in his bitterness, to reveal to us an army of fascists behind him ready for action. On what forces did he rely or think to rely? He had been cut off from the world for eight years, then, suddenly, freed: Can we believe that he had a clear idea of the situation? Between this hollow voice which was trailing along the air waves and the slaughters which were being carried out in the sewers, the Communist press has insisted on seeing a profound relationship. Those who have believed it have done so emotionally; only Stalinist paranoia prevents them from seeing the truth: the fact is that this old, isolated priest and these head-hunters are separated by an immense gap. The evolution of the Hungarian uprising depended on neither. I know the influence of the Church is deep: later, at the time of elections, who knows if Mindszenty wouldn't have bailed out the party of the counterrevolutionaries? Yes, who knows? But who knows whether his intransigence would not have worried Rome and turned most of the believers away from him? On this point, no one can decide; neither here, with the scanty news at our disposal, nor even in Budapest where the game wasn't played.

On the eve of the second aggression, in fact, Saturday, October 31, the positive elements were numerous. The bourgeois press and *L'Humanité* were together in wishing them away: the latter because it clings to its "Saint Bartholomew of the Patriots," the former because it insists on seeing in the Hungarian drama the admirable rebound of stifled liberalism. It is therefore necessary to emphasize them.

The countries of Central Europe do not all have the same structure: they are all having a rough go but they are not experiencing the same difficulties. After 1945, the Czech Government, for example, faced a serious problem: the progress of industry, between the two wars, had considerably developed the unproductive classes. They had to be integrated into the new society, to be reabsorbed little by little. I don't believe that they completely succeeded nor that this bourgeoisie ever rallied to the regime. It is educated, capable, potentially to be feared: it might very well turn to its own profit a national insurrection against the Communist leaders or transform it into civil war. It is true that, over there, the proletariat too is very strong. In any case, in Prague, the events would take another turn, even if they were to begin as in Budapest. The fact is that the prewar Hungarian bourgeoisie was hardly developed: far from constituting the preponderant social force, scarcely can we count it among the *ruling* classes. The *compradors* terrorized by the large property owners hadn't dared to carry out their "bourgeois revolution" nor to endow the country with a national industry. In contrast, they favored the development of foreign enterprises. Hungary found itself in the hands of the large landowners, its natural resources were being exploited by highly industrialized countries: it is with good cause that Fejtö calls it "a semi-colonial nation." The "tertiary" never developed there: the hostility of a national upper bourgeoisie leaning on the middle classes which it has developed, a plethora of high civil servants and administrators who, though wage earners, are entirely devoted to capital: that's the worst danger which a young socialist State can encounter, at its beginning.[1] The Hungarian State was spared this peril in advance. The upper bourgeoisie has always been slight and cosmopolitan: emigration and the purges took care of it, it has entirely disappeared; it wasn't to be feared that it would take over the controls nor that it would deflect the insurrec-

---

[1] The reader can profitably consult Stefan Heym's novel: *The Eyes of Reason* (*Les Yeux de la raison*). This German Communist recounts with a great deal of talent the conflicts of an important capitalist family with the Czech Government and with the workers, between 1945 and 1949. It will be said: "It's only a novel." Of course; but he makes a very shrewd and closely reasoned analysis of the social conflicts and the difficulties particular to postwar Czechoslovakia.

tion. The Hungarian petite bourgeoisie, composed of shop-keepers and artisans, certainly shows conservative tendencies; but in no case can these tendencies be compared to the will to exploit which characterizes a capitalist class; it's simply a matter of a profound devotion to individual ownership. There is no doubt that this small-scale ownership (of shops, of stores), still largely tolerated by the Hungarian leaders, can develop normally only in a society with a capitalist structure where the play of competition, favoring some at the expense of others, leads to concentration. But the point is this type of society had never been able to get established in Hungary; it is now, in any case, only a memory or a dream: where would one find the forces capable of reconstructing private capital? This petite bourgeoisie vegetates and clings to its last privilege more than it dreams of winning new advantages;[1] it remains under Rakosi what it was under Horthy: its "class viscosity" is so considerable that sons do not rise above their fathers, unless they become Communists and go into the Administration. What changes everything, indeed, is that there is, above it, a social group which possesses bourgeois comfort and power, which would be able to carry it along with it, perhaps: this is the socialist bureaucracy: power and wealth come to it from its adherence to a practice and an ideology which are still repugnant to the petits bourgeois. I have never considered the bureaucracy as a class. I even find this identification totally absurd: it none the less remains that the high civil servants and even the ordinary agents of the political police enjoyed scandalous privileges in Hungary. Thus, the Hungarian insur-

---

[1] Integrated into the system, controlled, buying and selling the merchandise furnished by the Government at fixed prices, the small shopkeeper looks very like the smallest unit of state-controlled distribution. But as long as the big "universal" stores are not multiplied, these sales posts will preserve a semblance of autonomy.

55

rection was raising up misery and want against opulence. It wasn't *primarily* the principle of private ownership which the petite bourgeoisie was defending alongside the workers. The contradiction of this reactionary class is that it was fighting against privileges and against luxury, in the name of the simple right to live. Thus, whatever its long-term and subjective aims, it was objectively defending a more equalitarian socialism alongside of socialists and against corrupted socialists.

As to the large landowners, they had emigrated: Had they wished to come back, thanks to the disorder, on what support could they count? The country people, at the announcement of the uprising, had redistributed the land of the cooperatives; they had, in sum, destroyed the socialist effort of the Revolution. But this liquidation didn't bring them back to 1939: these unfortunates—of whom the oldest had never worked, up to the war, except on others' land—found themselves landowners; they preserved the regime's first reform, this division of land which could be called "bourgeois." If the Nagy Government had consented to this Nep, if it had given its blessing to the failure of accelerated collectivization, not in order to stay indefinitely immobilized, but in order to begin socialization again slowly and prudently, the Hungarian peasants would have found themselves in the position of the recipients of national property at the time of the French Revolution; they would have defended the regime as our small landowners defended the Republic because they would have, like the French peasants, feared above all the return of the émigrés. Cardinal Mindszenty sensed this very well, since he began by declaring that he accepted without reserve the nationalization of Church property. Moreover, there were hardly any disturbances in the countryside: the Soviet troops were, for the most part, occupied in the large industrial centers; there is no mention of combat or massacre; merely a few settlings of accounts. After this new division of land, effected everywhere by unanimous consent, the peasants felt satisfied and went back to work. This new situation involved risks: the cooperatives do not propose only to increase productivity, they aim at preventing the reconstitution of the large landholdings. But this danger was long-term: a solidly established government could take measures, forbid the deeding and selling of land, hit the new kulaks with ruinous taxes. Against the forced collectivization, the Hungarian small landowner had allied himself with the kulaks; he will ally himself with the Government against the kulaks who ruin him in order to take his holdings from him: in both cases, he is fighting against expropriation.

In point of fact, the program of the insurgents was never reactionary. The total failure of the cooperatives certainly had to be rung up. It was right; it was politic.[1] But, at the Kilian barracks, during the conference of the insurrectional chiefs, one of them, a Communist, declared that the conquests of socialism would stick, no matter what happened; his motion received unanimous support. He had in view, obviously, the socialization of industry. Shortly afterwards, moreover, the insurrection forced Nagy to accept as point of departure a de facto regime which scandalized the Russians, but which

---

[1] It was right. The ill-will and the passive resistance of the collectivized peasants had this result in Hungary that the small-scale ownership, saddled with taxes and price rates, subject to the worst vexations, had— everything else being equal—a better yield in quantity and quality than the huge collectivized enterprises. The "about face" imposed itself then, first and foremost, from the simple economic point of view.

It was politic. In the face of an all-powerful opponent, the insurrection wanted to build the unity of the whole country. If the redistribution of land had not been ratified, the country people would have thought that the revolution was being made against them. In fact, thanks to the "United Front," of all the demands, the peasants helped the city insurgents. According to eyewitnesses, Budapest was never so well supplied with fresh provisions as during the last days of October.

Rakosi's faults had made necessary: the industrial sector would remain nationalized, the agricultural sector would be provisionally abandoned to small-scale private ownership. I have spoken of the dangers of this regime and I have demonstrated its necessity. The future was to depend on the parties and the men which the insurrection would bring to power.

Now, after the fake departure of Soviet troops, the Hungarian combatants looked to tightening their links. To prevent the resurrection of the former political formations or to limit the risks of an election, they envisaged forming a great party of the Revolution which would group the Christian right and the petite bourgeoisie, the ex-members of the Party of Small Property Owners, the Social-Democrats and the Communists. Negotiations were seriously underway when the Red Army made its so noted return. It was necessary to interrupt them to take up arms again. No one knows whether they would have succeeded; and, even in this case, no one can say whether this party would not have split apart. But, if it had been able to live with its contradictions, no doubt that it would have received the majority of votes. Socialism could have profited from it: in a Parliament elected on the basis of the 1945 elections, the C.P. and social-democracy would have found themselves in the minority confronting hostile and tight-shut parties, impermeable to their influence; they would have constituted the opposition—perhaps an ineffective opposition. On the other hand, within the great party of the Revolution, no barrier separated them from their former fighting comrades. Now they were the only ones possessing a know-how, a method, an ideology; they alone had a technique of propaganda and agitation at their disposal; they alone knew how to organize, administer; they alone aimed at distant goals beyond the immediate objectives: these incontestable superiorities

58

should allow them to exercise a decisive influence on hesitant and political inexperienced men.

As early as November 3, the union of the insurgents was bearing its first fruits and order was beginning to be re-established. It's at this precise moment that the Red Army chose to strike. How could one dare to claim that the tanks came back to Budapest to cope with a state of extreme emergency? The temporary anarchy which still reigned in this encircled city one can imagine didn't much bother the Kremlin. What preoccupied it above all, was the further development of the situation and its repercussions. Now, there is no doubt that the return to calm would have been the beginning of a hard struggle; the contradictions of an economy torn between the socialized industrial sector and the "free" agricultural sector would have rapidly set the cities against the countries, workers against peasants; the question of food supply and of prices would have posed itself immediately: regulating the price of food products would have aroused the anger of the farm people; not regulating prices would have starved the worker. The middle class would have taken advantage of this conflict to set itself up as arbiter; but it carried within it its own contradictions: city-dwelling, it had the same needs as the proletariat, an authoritarian policy on food supply and prices would have served its interests; conservative, it would have allied itself with the rural classes to defend private property. In the countryside—as I have already said—much tact and skill would have been needed to prevent the new kulaks from exploiting or expropriating the poor; on the cultural front, Marxism, still powerful but a bit discredited, would have run up against alternative ideologies generously offered by the West and, who knows, against a sudden resurgence of the Christian faith. It is to the totality of these conflicts and not to the cock-and-bull stories of *L'Humanité* that the name of "class struggle" must be given. Workers, petits bourgeois, peasants, kulaks, and small landowners: it is on the collision of these forces, on the complex play of their alliances, and, of course, on relations with the U.S.S.R. and the West, that the fate of Hungary could have hung. But then? Isn't it on these very things that it hangs today and will hang tomorrow? The Russians can do nothing about it. Had the class struggle ceased, under Rakosi? Wasn't the withering of the cooperatives a result of it? Had the hold of Christianity been loosened? And did the workers, in spite of the disgust they were filled with, cease for a moment to want socialism? Irritation and the magnitude of dangers can bring people together briefly, brute force can stamp out differences for a time: one must always come back to politics, wade into an uncertain undertaking, take risks, trust certain classes and lean on them. The Soviets have always underestimated the revolutionary power of workers' movements; in the Hungarian affair, they immediately noted the shift towards the Right and were unable to distinguish the simultaneous reinforcement of the Left: distrust is not dialectic. Nor is Manicheism. The Soviet bureaucracy doesn't like workers in arms; it far and away prefers soldiers. On November 4, it bet against the Marxist revolutionaries in favor of the triumph of the counterrevolution. The struggle which was beginning, it is true could have, perhaps, ended in civil war, but it would have led quite as well to the true dictatorship of the proletariat. For the working class was armed; and it was to keep its arms: the insurgents wanted to form, after the departure of the Russians, a National Guard composed of students and workers. They would have been made, in sum, the guardians of nationalized industry. What power they would have been given against the émigrés and the counterrevolutionaries, these men whom the

Russian armored vehicles didn't intimidate. After the crushing of the insurrection, on November 16, over Radio-Budapest, could be heard a representative of the Factory Committees who was asking his comrades to go back to work conditionally. He spoke as a conqueror, with an admirable pride: they would stop the strike to come to the aid of the inhabitants of Budapest; they would start it again at once if the demands of the strikers were not satisfied. And he had this to say, in a building crammed full of cops, in the middle of a ravaged city where Russian tanks were patrolling: "The whole world knows our strength." We know it, it's true: a million, six hundred thousand workers are holding in check the most powerful of armies. Do people believe that those men would not have been capable by themselves of stamping out the counter-revolution? Of course it was necessary to take risks, to organize, to define a policy, to seek alliances: they were ready to do it. Was it then so mad a project? And which was better for the Country of the Workers: to gut a capital, decimate a population, ruin an economy already near bankruptcy, or to place confidence in a conscious, armed proletariat? A struggle had to be anticipated, yes, but it was a *true* struggle, that of the real forces of Hungary; the class conflict would have broken out in the open! Doubtless, but what is gained by hiding it? The U.S.S.R. would have looked on, helpless, at the crushing of the forces of the Left. Why? Couldn't it favor them? Grant a substantial aid to a government in which the Communists were strongly represented? Nothing is served by arresting the free development of a country by force: it is up to it to overcome its contradictions. But, one will say, the émigrés? the commandos? the West? Come now! The U.S.S.R. has just crushed the Hungarian resistance and not one western country budged. A distinguished speaker was saying just the other day, at the Peace Movement: "Why bother with Hungary? No one will wage war for the Hungarians." This speaker was a progressive and the Communists applauded him. So? Do people believe that the U.S.S.R. was unable to negotiate with the U.S.A.? To compel the total neutrality of the West in exchange for its own? To declare that it would hold the Western powers responsible for the armed groups which would be organized on their territory and which would try to cross the Hungarian border? To proclaim that it would send two hundred thousand "volunteers"—as it did for Suez—in the case that armed émigrés entered Hungary? The Western blabbermouths got themselves detested by the Hungarians whom they pushed to revolt only to abandon them afterwards to their fate: however strong the anti-Sovietism, couldn't the U.S.S.R. count on the anti-Westernism? By withdrawing its troops, wouldn't it have regained—at least in part—the ground lost? Ah! that was taking risks. Yes. But does one imagine, by chance, that one doesn't take greater ones still by having recourse to force?

No one has the right to say that the events in Hungary made the intervention inevitable. No one; not even those who decided it. Besides, the blunders and the repentances, the false starts, the returns,[1] this strange paralysis of troops in the face of the strike, the announcement of the deportations broadcast by Radio-Budapest itself and denied the next day, the strange coming and going of trains crammed with prison-

---

[1] Negotiations were still going on in Budapest between Russian and Hungarian military elements when the order to attack was given. Our anticommunists didn't miss this chance to stress Soviet perfidy. I don't believe in this perfidy: and first of all the very power of the means brought into play made it unnecessary. It seems rather that different groups in the Kremlin were seeking the solution to the Hungarian affair at the same time and by independent paths. Finally, the partisans of repression won out.

ers who were being taken towards the border "to be interrogated" and subsequently brought back, the "shift to the Right" of the Kadar Government which seemed for a moment to embrace all Nagy's concessions (except neutralization), then its sudden hardening, the deportation of Nagy and his Ministers, the pure and simple rejection of the workers' demands, soon followed by a reopening of negotiations, then by the dissolution of the Committees:[1] all this goes to show the Soviet hesitations. No: we are not dealing with the upsurge of a popular power suddenly backed into a corner and faced with using violence or accepting the irreparable: we are witnessing the incoherent action, now feeble, now brutal and hasty, of a disunited government which is bogged down in its internal divisions, in its own ideology, which gets disconcerted faced with the attitude of its soldiers and discovers in amazement, but too late, the truth which its lackeys hide from it. What made the intervention inevitable is not the White Terror in Budapest, it's the triumph of a certain policy in Moscow. They would have us believe that it was necessary on the face of it and for universally valid reasons (that is to say, capable of being accepted by all men of the Left). It's not true: some men, by placing themselves *in a certain political perspective*, based on an evaluation *which is their own* of the international situation, judged it preferable to refuse the socialist forces of the new Hungary their chances and to plunge this country into chaos. Never were the events in Budapest judged in and of themselves: they were envisaged only by the repercussions they could have in Central Europe and, in the end, on the two blocs.

---

[1] These are the Committees which Kadar wishes to reconstitute today with the same elected representatives and with respect to which he asserts the Gerö Government was thinking of organizing them *before October 23*, while Pravda condemns their existence—in Yugoslavia.

Whoever will believe, indeed, that the Soviets sought, in Hungary, to defend Hungarian socialism? If they thought they were doing so, what naïveté and what a failure! What did they win? Nothing. What did they lose? Everything. They kindled in peoples' hearts a hatred which is far from dying out and which serves reaction. They disqualified the Hungarian Party forever and forced it to repudiate itself by changing its name. They succeeded in ruining the economy and when, to reconstruct it, the active collaboration of the whole people would be needed, they raised the masses up against the Government. They put in power a national Communist whose popularity could have served them, but they discredited him in advance by obliging him to take upon himself the responsibility for the massacres. They provoked a general strike of protest which singles out for the whole world the Red Army, the Army of the Workers, as the enemy of the Hungarian workers. They don't dare have recourse to force openly to bring the workers back in the factories, and yet they multiply the arrests. They can't leave without having the peoples' anger sweep out the leaders which have been imposed upon them, nor stay without condemning Kadar's only resource, democratization, to remain a dead issue. Caught in their own trap, they are bogged down in an occupation which I hope their troops hold in horror and which is justified a bit more every day by the harm it is doing and the resentment it is engendering. Violence and oppression are progressively moving this martyred country away from the socialist camp; to keep it there, they have only one means left: oppression and violence. Before this month of October, they were winning across the boards, they were coming out victors of the cold war, they were having a reconciliation with Tito and restoring the unity of the socialist camp, they were extending their influence as far as India and the Middle East; in the bourgeois democracies, their cultural offensive was bearing fruit, the Twentieth Congress was disarming the propaganda of the adversary. Today, Nehru condemns them, the Afro-Asian countries are hesitant, worried, *Pravda* and *Borba* are exchanging insults; the Budapest massacres have destroyed years of efforts for detente, for coexistence, for peace; never, in the West, have the Communists found themselves more isolated, never has their confusion been greater, never has the Right triumphed so noisily. All that, one could foresee; in the dark days of November 2 and 3, when the radio was announcing the entrance of Soviet reinforcements into Hungary, the men of the Left, the friends of the U.S.S.R. and Communists, in France and everywhere, were weighing the consequences of a *coup de force* and were saying to themselves: It's not possible, they won't do it.

They did it. But in the name of what, and what did they want to save? The answer is simple: Those who were responsible for the intervention acted in the conviction that a world conflict was inevitable, the politics from which they take their cue is the politics of the blocs and the cold war.

Where it comes from, what objectives it pursues, which men put it into practice, what its significance is for socialism, this is what I must now establish.

In our bourgeois countries, people know what had to be paid to carry through "primitive accumulation"; people haven't forgotten the tremendous waste of human lives, the forced labor, the misery, the revolts, the repression. It seems that the industrialization of the U.S.S.R. cost less; what a terrible effort it required, however; how much sweat, how much blood: it was a race against the clock, in an underdeveloped country, almost entirely agricultural, encircled, which had to develop itself in spite of an economic blockade and under the constant threat of an armed aggression. No one will ever be able to say to what point this "besieged fortress" could, without risking total destruction, reduce the suffering and hardships of its inhabitants; what is sure is that the Communist leaders assumed the entire responsibility for the regime in its greatness and in its defects. The bourgeois liberal pleads not-guilty: it's not he who made the world; he, like everyone, obeys the inexorable laws of the economy; but the Soviet revolutionaries, after some years of uncertainty, finally understood that socialism was not separable from economic planning. Moreover, the urgency of the dangers and the lack of culture of the masses made it necessary for the Russian Government to declare itself for an authoritarian planning; whereupon, the leaders became assimilated with the Plan itself, the Plan took on their faces, their voices and their hands, it became the real Government. This alienation of the head office from the enterprise could only accentuate the major contradiction of Soviet society: the long-term interests of socialist construction were opposed to the immediate interests of the working class. In a bourgeois democracy, indeed, the proletariat is per se, as Marx says: "the decomposition of society *qua* single class." In this negative situation, there is such an assimilation of its immediate reactions into its historical task that it is the masses which set the example for radicalism: their spontaneous demands result in accelerating the dissolution of capitalist society, at the same time that they express the basic character of the proletarians, "the secret of their own existence." Thus, the oppressed class has "a universal character through its universal sufferings" and Marx can use the word "oughtness" (*devoir*), which he borrows from ethics, to characterize demands whose origin is immediate self-interest. In other terms, the needs of the worker, in a capitalist regime, his fatigue, his hunger, for example, have a socialist character in their very nakedness: the results of exploitation, these needs cannot be asserted without putting exploitation in question, they cannot be satisfied without diminishing profit and endangering capital. But, in Soviet Russia, the major concern of the leaders will be to achieve the material conditions which will permit the resolution of problems which the Revolution created. Now, the spontaneous reactions of the masses keep their negative character in relation to the general needs of the economy. In the period of post-revolutionary construction, at the moment when the socialist State wishes to endow the country with an industrial setup, the movement of the masses in the direction of their demands threatens to compromise everything: the worker can refuse intensive work, demand a wage increase, clothing, shoes, a housing program. In a word, his immediate interest brings him to call for the development of consumer industries in a society which will perish if it does not first provide itself with heavy industry. Universal in a bourgeois society, his demand becomes particular in a post-revolutionary society: however his situation hasn't changed; it's true that he is no longer exploited, but "the contradiction between his human *nature* and his real life existence" has not disappeared: the Revolution, whatever it may be, does not work miracles, it inherits the misery which the *Ancien Régime* produced. Of course, this conflict does not limit itself to setting the Plan, the necessary condition for progress towards socialism, against the worker as labor power and a system of needs. It exists in both: for the worker wants the achievement of socialism at the same time as the satisfaction of his needs. In the name of the first, he is willing to restrict the second; one can ask great sacrifices of him. But, a shift in his objectives takes place: in a capitalist regime, he was aiming at the overthrow of the bourgeoisie and the dictatorship of the proletariat through and beyond his concrete demands: the long-range goals made sense of the immediate needs, the immediate needs gave a *real* content to these goals. The worker was in agreement with himself, and the leaders, while *organizing* the movement of the masses, couldn't escape their control: the leaders could lead the masses only where they wished to go. In a period of post-revolutionary construction, the worker's socialism rests on a solid base: the socialization of the means of production.[1] He knows that his efforts must sooner or later profit the working class itself and, through it, the whole population; work no longer appears to him as a hostile force, but as a concrete link among the different social milieus. A rational understanding of the situation and of its necessities, the desire not to compromise what has been achieved, faithfulness to principles, to the goal: all this predisposes him to restrict his needs as much as he can, to consider his fatigue as an individual happening which concerns only him, whereas he used to see in it, at the time of bourgeois exploitation, the expression of a universal fatigue of his class. All the same his socialist goals no longer are seen through the lived necessity which was the grounds for his demands; even if he wants to work more in order to free his sons from the constraint of needs, it's to his sons' needs that he ties the progress of industrialization and not to his own. It is not certain that this divorce would have been so clear if the Revolution of October 1917 had broken out in Germany or in England, rather than in Russia: in these

---

[1] Even after the failure of the planned economies, in Hungary and in Poland the proletariat considers it has won something which it is ready to defend by arms: in neither country has it put socialism in question or allowed it to be put in question. It's a *policy* which it denounces (in Hungary it goes so far as to condemn the Party which is responsible for this policy), but it remains faithful to the regime.

already industrialized countries, the rhythm and the allocation of investments would have been of another nature. But since the U.S.S.R. must *before everything* else provide itself with machinery, it will take a long time before the efforts and sacrifices of each one has a *visible* result of raising the standard of living. This real dichotomy of the worker in the first phase of socialist construction is curiously highlighted, in new Poland, by the coexistence, for some enterprises, of management councils and union setups elected by the same workers. Bourdet asked if these organisms didn't overlap; the workers told him no: "The management council, although emanating directly from us, is moved along by the general process of the economy; it represents us in our national universality as socialist workers and as such might well underestimate our concrete needs and immediate interests; it's for this reason that unions are necessary." Thus, the socialist contradiction carries with it the necessity for the same workers to have a double representation: the permanent opposition between the management council and the union only recapitulates in the broad daylight of objectivity the conflict which each lives through darkly. Perhaps this objectification will go beyond the contradiction: in the U.S.S.R., in the heroic times of the first five-year plans, it was inconceivable. The proletariat was daily swollen by a mass of illiterate peasants whom the requirements of concentration were tearing away from the fields; the civil war had decimated the workers' elite; these confused masses, without political education, do not have a clear awareness of their tasks and their future; the conflict of the universal and the particular exists in them only in an embryonic state; overworked, underfed, they are distinguished above all by their needs. The contradiction is clearly seen, on the other hand, at the level of the leaders, but it appears above all as a problem to be resolved within the framework of the Plan: the human needs appear as a factor of primary importance, but a negative factor, which tends to slow down production. It is humane, it is politic to make the largest concessions to them, having taken into account the vital needs of the Soviet economy. In this first phase, the masses lose the power of pointing the finger themselves at their own needs; it is the experts who decide what is suitable for them. In a pre-revolutionary period, the cadres and the apparatus—however authoritarian—remained under the control of the working classes; after the Revolution, the socialist experiment partially escapes from this *human* control, it tends to substitute technical criteria for it. Forced to *figure out* the objective contradictions of the economic movement, the leaders become detached from the workers' condition; they are all pure discernment of objectivity and authoritarian action which resolves difficulties. Thus the mass becomes a passive and unconscious object of historical contradictions while the leaders decide investments, rates of work and the standard of living by a veritable "rational calculation."

About the same time, industrialization engenders a population upheaval which requires increasing agricultural productivity. These changes suddenly make apparent the contradictions which oppose the workers to the rural inhabitants: the former can compensate for the inadequacy of their wages only by a lowering and authoritarian stabilization of agricultural prices; the latter demand that the lowering of prices be on manufactured products. The government sees itself obliged to achieve rural collectivization by constraint: large-scale operations have a better yield and are easier to control. The working class unreservedly supports this strong-arm policy of violence which serves the interests of urban concentrations; besides, the industrial workers consider the nationalization of industries as

70

the greatest victory of the proletariat: agrarian collectivization appears to them as a necessary consequence of the socialization of industry. The rural inhabitants, on the contrary, even if they belong to a prosperous kolkhoz, do not cease to resist what they consider to be an expropriation. In fact both were put under the unconditional authority of the Plan: it is none the less true that the demands of construction created the conditions for a veritable class struggle between workers and peasants and that this struggle became exacerbated to the point of becoming a civil war; deportations and executions cannot suppress this struggle: from 1930 on, the Soviet leaders are compelled to exercise in the name of the proletariat an iron dictatorship on a hostile peasantry.

Stalinism was born of this double contradiction. At first the Plan engenders its own instruments: it develops a bureaucracy of experts, technicians and administrators as rationalization, in capitalist countries, develops the "tertiary" sector.[1] It is absurd to pretend that this bureaucracy *exploits* the proletariat and that it is a *class*, or then words no longer have meaning. And it isn't true either that its only concern is to defend its own interests. Its members are much too well paid but they wear themselves out on the job; they put in more hours at work than the workers. Born of the Plan, it is the Plan which legitimatizes their privileges: their personal ambition is not distinct from their devotion to socialism conceived as abstract economic planning, that is to say, ultimately, as the continuous increase of production. This total alienation allows them to consider themselves as organs of the universal to the extent that the Plan must be established by their efforts; the demands of the masses, on the contrary, even if they take them into ac-

---

[1] To the extent that it cut the leaders off from the masses, it necessarily develops the only power which can assure its realization: the police.

count, are for them particular accidents of a strictly negative character. And, in point of fact, their situation is contradictory in itself, for it is true that they represent the universal to the extent that they seek to involve the entire country in the building of socialism, and it is also true that they represent a simple *particularism* to the extent that their function has cut them off from the Russian people and their concrete lives. Between these "organizers" and the masses, the Party claims to play the role of mediator. In fact, it constantly keeps the bureaucracy in line. By incessant persecutions, by reorganizations and "purges," it keeps it in suspense and prevents it from getting entrenched. But the Party is, in itself, the political expression of economic planning; creator of myths, specialized in propaganda, it controls, stirs up, exhorts the masses, it can unite them for a moment in a unanimous movement, but no more than the unions does it reflect their immediate interests, their demands nor the currents which keep them in ferment. The working classes close in on themselves and their real life falls into a kind of clandestinity: this estrangement engenders a reciprocal distrust. The leaders will ask themselves much later (they were putting the question to themselves in 1954, when I was in Moscow) how to interest the masses *as such* in production; but one formulates problems only when one has the means to resolve them. Today, the extraordinary progress of the Soviet economy permits envisaging real solutions: in a capitalist regime, the revolutionary movement is characterized by the profound unity of its long-term objectives and of its immediate goals, but this unity defines it as a negativity; at a certain stage of socialization the development of the Soviet economy can facilitate the unification of popular objectives in a positive process of construction. But in the period which follows the Revolution, the prerevolutionary unity gives way to an insurmountable contradiction. It becomes necessary then to create a workers' elite for whom the increase in productivity will express itself in a material improvement and who will find its most immediate interest in the fulfillment and overfulfillment of the Plan. This connection between immediate well-being and the building of socialism is perfectly artificial: it is achieved by arbitrary authority, and for a few by drawing on the available surplus value. These "heroes of labor" are cited everywhere as an example, but the example is false; their small number is the very condition of their prosperity; at the same time, their existence alone is enough to carry along with it, sometimes without the knowledge of the masses, a general raising of norms. The necessities of socialization predispose the leaders to underestimate the revolutionary force of the proletariat; they work on it from the outside by propaganda, by a diffuse constraint, by emulation and in any case they prefer the Stakhanovites who were born of the Plan like them and like them are sold on the increase in production. On their side, the working masses stick with the regime, but they don't have confidence in the bureaucracy. Certainly, between an alienated bureaucracy and a crushed peasantry, the industrial workers are the only ones to keep a certain independence and even— within well-defined limits—a certain right to criticize. It is none the less true that they feel governed from the outside. The proletariat is no longer the subject of history, it is not yet the concrete goal of socialization: it feels itself to be the *principal object* of administrative solicitude and the *essential means* of socialist construction. Precisely because of that, socialism remains its class "duty" and ceases to be its reality. Meanwhile, the bureaucracy hounds itself and relentlessly pursues its unification. The contradictions of socialism and, quite particularly, the conflict between the proletariat and the peasants, compel the leaders to take abrupt tacks, to change direction endlessly, and endlessly to correct the prior changes. The existence of a rightist faction and a leftist faction within the administration would cause economic planning to run the gravest risks: from what should be only a tactical retreat or a temporary toughening, the victory of *one* policy would be claimed, that is to say, the victory of one team and one program. In point of fact, the Plan is only a hypothesis constantly submitted to the control of experience and which one should be able to correct, without any other bias, in the light of the experience itself. The urgency of the corrections entails total agreement among the organizers; this agreement alone will prevent the momentary change of direction from becoming fixed, from changing into an *orientation*; it alone will allow the revocation of any detrimental measure, even the one which has just been decided upon; alone it makes possible the leaders' constant submission to objectivity. Elsewhere, threats from abroad are becoming more explicit; and then the mute and hostile mass of rural inhabitants refuses to be rallied; it is necessary to put the accent on constraint; now a dictatorial group must first of all practice its dictatorship on itself. Thus, the the danger from without and the resistance from within require the indissoluble unity of the leaders. Without deep roots, without real support, the group of "organizers" will preserve its authority and assure the national security only if it first of all achieves *from within*, by itself and over itself, its own security; events oblige it to push its own integration to the limit. But the limit is never attained, for it is the biological and mental unity of the person which provides the best pattern for it. From this results this strange contradiction: each person becomes suspect in the eyes of everyone else and even in his own by the very reason that his unity frustrates complete assimilation; but *only* a person is capable of becoming the example, the agent, and the ideal end product of a social process of unification. At the very moment when each individual considers himself unessential in relation to the group taken as a whole, this whole must remain a simple operative symbol or the multiplicity of men must go beyond itself and unite in the sacred unity of an essential individual. Thus the cult of personality is above all else the cult of social unity in one person. And Stalin's function (*office*) is not to represent the indissolubility of the group, but *to be* this very indissolubility and, at the same time, to forge it. No one can be surprised to see this idolatry surge up in a regime which denounces and rejects bourgeois individualism, because it is precisely the product of this rejection; each bourgeois resembles all the others in that he insists on his particular difference and on the worth of his own person; these primitive affirmations balance each other; the apparent reciprocity of the relationships universalizes them; the bourgeois respects in himself and claims to respect in others the absolute dignity of the human being. Consequently, this cult lapses into abstraction; each being sacred, none is. Under the cover of this respect, the realistic appraisal of oneself and of others will depend on the particular content of this universal form: capabilities, actions, character. These material elements can constitute the object of a hierarchy, but not of a cult: none of them is valued a priori. Therefore, individualism excludes all possibility of idolatry. The successful artist, the star and the V.I.P., indispensable accessories of bourgeois ceremonies, certainly do not function to demonstrate the absolute superiority over everyone else; in everyone's eyes they incarnate his own possibilities; laden with honor, at the pinnacle of glory and power, their existence does more than the cleverest propaganda: contrary to all truth, it gives the impression that the highest positions are accessible to the humblest citizens. The function—as abstract power—is identified with the personality as pure form; this entity constitutes the object of the cult, it is sacred; but the *real* qualities of the individual aren't in it: every slightly pretty girl respects the star in Brigitte Bardot but remains persuaded that the qualities of this actress cannot entirely justify her eminence. There is such a lag between the concrete individual and what I will call the "personality function" that chance alone can lead the former to turn into the latter; now chance *is nothing*; thus every famous artist reflects for all the women of France their own possibilities of becoming sacred.[1]

By subordinating his person to the group, the Soviet man avoids the absurd vices of bourgeois personalism. But, by the same token, the ever more imperious necessity to maintain and reinforce unity causes his individual reality to go underground; despite the Constitution, this reality is deprived of status and remains only a factor of multiplicity, the possible source of a disunion, and the object of a latent distrust. The fights, however atrocious, remain in the realm of objectivity: they are solutions and projects in opposition to each other, but ambition and the affirmation of self remain implicit, they never appear in the light of day; the Plan covers and absorbs them. For lack of manifesting themselves, individual wills can neither recognize themselves nor balance each other in a system which would be a universal guarantee against all hypertrophy of the cult of personality. Actually, Stalin does not

---

[1] Bourgeois propaganda skillfully stresses the fact that public men, prestigious in their functions, have an ordinary private life like all lives. They are shown at home, celebrating with their wives (a very modest celebration), playing with their children. Their life story is told, showing them in their youth, ambitious, champing at the bit, like all young men when, suddenly, opportunity . . . ! Thus, in his development as in his private life, the leader, the V.I.P., the successful artist is *myself plus chance*.

appear at first as an individual superior to others but fundamentally like all. It is not the dignity of the person which he represents, it is social integration pushed to the limit. This indissolubility—which *happens* to be that of the individual—makes him the sole possible agent of unification, for it is unity alone which can unify multiplicity. He is identified with the coercive action which the group exercises on its own members; he will carry out the sentence which the bureaucracy passes on itself; he picks up and interiorizes the diffuse distrust of the revolutionary collectivity. In the name of all, he will be distrustful of each; but the group is not distrustful of him; within the bureaucracy, he would have represented only plurality and division; placed above it, he shows it as the reflection of impossible collective unity. Stalin's right hand does not distrust his left hand nor his left ear his right ear. Stalin cannot become the spy of Stalin nor cease to be in accord with himself. The group cannot continue to exist without confidence, it is not enough to say that it trusts Stalin, but it places its own confidence in the confidence which Stalin has in himself. No one *enjoys* this confidence except Stalin in person; but each one knows that up there, in Stalin, the bureaucratic collectivity exists under a form of superior integration and that it is reconciled. Thus each member of the bureaucracy, far from seeing in Stalin an exaltation of the human person, discovers in this quintessence of collectivity the radical negation of his own self to the profit of unity. The ascending movement which goes from the group to Stalin is characterized then by the total destruction of individuality. On the other hand, there is a descending movement: Stalin can resolve the problem of integration only by pushing social hierarchy to the limit. From the top to the bottom of the ladder, directly or indirectly, the officials get their power from him. Thus one sees the rebirth of the *person*. But the latter has nothing in common with the bourgeois individual. It does not derive its existence from a universal status, but from the unique person whom the necessities of integration place above the group. Its reality, always revokable, comes to it from its very functions; in its relations with its peers, it remains a factor of multiplicity, hence an object of distrust; for its subordinates, on the other hand, it is a hypostasis of Stalin, hence a factor of unification and an object of worship. At all levels of the hierarchy, we find the same contradiction; biological and mental autonomy appears as the element of plurality and as a symbol of integration; the same individual presents himself as a synthesizing force vis-a-vis his subordinates and denies his living reality in his relationships with his chiefs. In any case, what sets up and what destroys the Soviet person is the impossible unity of the group. Stalin, alone, is pure unity: he is the act. It is not his own individual qualities which are worshiped in him; even less, some kind of "charismatic" power like that which the Nazis recognized in Hitler. His cult has nothing mystical; it is directed to a real unity in so far as it is a power of unification. It is inseparable moreover from terror: Stalin incarnating the collective distrust can overcome multiplicity only by trying to reduce it. The negative counterpart of hierarchization is this circulating terror which the bureaucracy practices on itself by Stalin's hands and which expresses itself by "purges" and deportations.

"Socialism in a single country," or Stalinism, does not constitute a deviation from socialism: it is the long way around which is imposed on it by circumstances. The rhythm and evolution of this defensive construction are not determined by the consideration alone of Soviet resources and needs but also by the relations of the U.S.S.R. with the capitalist world, in a word, by circumstances external to socialization which oblige it constantly to compromise its principles. The contradictions of this first phase provoke a class conflict between workers and peasants and cut off the leaders from the working masses: an authoritarian and bureaucratic system is established where everything is sacrificed to productivity. This system reflects its contradictions in its ideological superstructures: it appeals to Marxism-Leninism but this wrapper ill-conceals a double-value judgment on man and on socialism. On the one hand, the propaganda and the Pollyanna novels of "socialist realism" appeal to a quite nauseating optimism: in a socialist country everything is good, there is no conflict except between the forces of the past and those which are building the future; the latter must necessarily triumph. The failures, suffering, death, all are caught up and saved by the movement of history. It even seems opportune for a while to produce novels without conflicts. In any case, the positive hero knows nothing about internal difficulties and contradictions; for his part, he contributes, without flinching and without mistakes, to the construction of socialism, his model is the young Stakhanovite; a soldier, he knows nothing of fear. These industrial and military idylls appeal to Marxism: they depict for us the happiness of a classless society. On the other hand, the exercise of dictatorship and the internal contradictions of bureaucracy necessarily engender an unavowed pessimism: since one governs by force, men must be evil; these heroes of labor, these so devoted high functionaries, these Party militants so upright, so pure, a mere puff can blow out their most blazing virtues: there they are counterrevolutionaries, spies, agents of capitalism; habits of integrity, of honesty, thirty years of faithfulness to the C.P., nothing can protect them against temptation. And if they deviate from the line, one soon discovers that they were guilty *from birth*. The great actions which merited for them so many honors and so much praise, one discovers suddenly, were heinous crimes: one had to be ready to revoke all judgments, to scorn the man whom one praised to the skies without ever being surprised at having been mistaken so long: in this dark and mixed up world, one must affirm all the more strongly today's truth for the fact that it will very likely be tomorrow's error. The State, far from withering away, must reinforce itself: its withering away will come when an authoritarian education has interiorized in everyone the constraints which the State practices; it is not the emancipation of men which will succeed in making it unnecessary, it is their self-domestication and their internal conditioning: it will not disappear, it will move into peoples' hearts. It is this distrust of man which is expressed in Stalin's famous "theoretical error": the class struggle is intensified in a period of socialist construction. It has been claimed that he wished cynically to justify his "practice." Why? It is practice, here, which engenders its own theory. Besides, this pessimism turns up in foreign policy. The U.S.S.R. doesn't want war but it sees it coming: for good reason, since Hitler's armies were to invade it in 1941. But these perfectly justifiable fears carry with them a gross over-simplification of problems: the capitalist world, out of reach, ill-known, becomes a purely destructive force which mercilessly pursues the extermination of the Soviet people and the liquidation of socialism by force of arms; people still talk of the contradictions of the capitalist world, of the conflicts which they can entail, of the peace forces which oppose the war forces in the West. People talk about them but they no longer believe in them, particularly after the failure of the Popular Front: for the only certain policy, in the state of isolation in which socialist Russia finds itself, is to arm, to arm ceaselessly *as if war were coming tomorrow*: thus foreign and domestic policy must be determined constantly in view of the risks of catastrophe, never in view of the chances of peace. So long as it has not caught up with the Western nations, the U.S.S.R. must remain faithful to the pessimistic principle: If you want peace, prepare for war (*Si vis pacem, para bellum*), which in French means: "You can always count on the worst" (*Le pire est toujours sûr*).

Must one give the name of socialism to this bloody monster which tears itself apart? I answer frankly: yes. It even was *the* socialism in its primitive phase, there was no other, except perhaps in Plato's heaven, and one had to have that one or not have any. The U.S.S.R.'s failure came to it, in 1945, from its victory: at Yalta it obtained a zone of influence which, for the first time, put it in a position to exercise its hegemony over a group of foreign nations. Up to that point, obsessed by the fear of encirclement, this enormous continental power, closed in on itself, cyst-like, had sought salvation only through superarmament and in the tightening of its internal ties. It had never felt the need nor found the occasion to provide itself with organs which would have permitted extending its influence outside: the war itself, it had won on its own soil by a kind of self-contraction. It came out of its isolation warily and Stalin feared this decisive test for his soldiers: contact with the West.[1] The U.S.S.R. demanded the friendship of these forced but necessary allies, but they inspired in it only distrust: some were yesterday's enemies; most offered the image of its former structure: lots of peasants, few workers; in

---

[1] He was convinced, Russians told me, that there would be a wave of desertions. But man does not always justify the mistrust of the pessimists: no one deserted. The soldiers brought back new techniques, suggestions, criticisms, a changed vision of the world but it didn't even occur to them to question the regime.

Rumania, in Hungary, no Communists. Besides, it didn't have much use for the workers, Communists or not, outside of its own country: during the 1920s, it had too ardently hoped for world revolution not to bear bitterness towards the European proletariats for not having carried it out. In the beginning the no man's land (*glacis*) had only a military interest; the Red Army took the responsibility of carrying out the Revolution everywhere: it was not a question then of exporting socialism but of creating popular regimes which, in defending the U.S.S.R., would defend themselves. Coalition governments were constituted everywhere in which the Communists, often in the minority, had only a hidden influence.

It is the Marshall Plan which changed everything. This war maneuver revealed a disquieting truth: the United States could immediately come to the aid of these poor or ruined countries, the U.S.S.R. did not yet have the means to outfit them. The political solidarity which had just been established with much difficulty would not weigh heavily against the economic solidarity which the West was proposing; already the hesitations of Czechoslovakia showed the fragility of the system. Incapable of taking up the challenge, the Soviet Government had to give up its allies or hold on to them by force. It chose to tighten its grip, to assure the dictatorship of the Communists everywhere and to launch all the "satellites" into the construction of socialism.

It was perfectly right: at the time the relationship of forces was unfavorable to the U.S.S.R.; the satellites' return to a capitalist regime would have represented for it the rebirth and aggravation of encirclement: before 1939, Central Europe was eating itself away: in each country minority ethnic groups, in perpetual effervescence, constituted a permanent danger of separatism and civil war; conflicts of interest, rivalries or ancient hatreds set each of them against all the others. Paralyzed by its dissensions, this broad region full of still unexploited riches was above all the passive stake in the struggle which opposed German imperialism and the Western democracies. The U.S.S.R. could be threatened through it but not by it. After 1945, the situation had entirely changed: the crushing of Germany created a vacuum in Europe, the Soviet people had raised up the small nations with their own hands, the war had put a brake on ethnic and national rivalries. In each country, a strong power had achieved a true unity for the first time: if they escaped Russian control, the Peoples Democracies, nourished, equipped, armed by the United States, would become on the Russian frontier the advanced borders of the enemy. This direct and active threat made the position of the Soviet Union still more difficult than in the time of Hitler's Germany. No one seriously imagined that they could remain neutral. Neutrality depends on the historical conjuncture: today, the relationship of forces tends towards equilibrium; it is therefore no longer absurd that certain nations, in certain circumstances, call for a neutrality status guaranteed by all the powers. Nor that peoples urgently demand the end of the cold war and of the "blocs." In 1948, the danger came from a lack of equilibrium: no State could spare itself the barren and painful effort which would one day end up in re-establishing the equality of military potentials. The Red Army was in the heart of Europe, Berlin. America had partially disarmed but it was daily increasing its stock of atomic weapons. The U.S.A. feared a classical war which would carry Russian soldiers all the way to the edge of the Atlantic; the U.S.S.R. feared perishing in the course of a new war with unforeseen developments, conducted by technicians, at long distance, with weapons of which the West had secured an actual monopoly. This reciprocity of terror was cutting the world in two: one stuck to one of the energy fields only to be grabbed by the other. In this conjuncture, the Marshall Plan appears as a provocation: under its peaceful exterior, it was the come on of a policy of "roll-back." Since the Russians did not yet have the means to combat this economic penetration on its own terrain, they were reduced to opposing it by constraint. They were losing on all counts: the U.S.S.R. let its weakness be seen; a clever propaganda was accusing it, even within the Peoples Democracies, of responding by *coup de force* to the disinterested offer of the United States and of egotistically depriving the underdeveloped countries of an aid which was indispensable to them. The Russian leaders saw the trap and did not hesitate to take on their responsibilities. In its principle, their policy was correct: by the pressure which they exerted on their allies, they were safeguarding peace, the construction of socialism in the U.S.S.R., *they could also preserve in Central Europe the chances for socialization.*

On the condition of undertaking this socialization *in the interest* of the small nations, in taking into account their situation, their needs and their resources, the social structures, the internal resistances. It was necessary and possible to avoid for them the terrible experiences of the Soviet Union; now it is precisely that which the Russian leaders refused to understand. Legitimately proud of their tragic and grandiose history, did they really believe that the other nations had only to reproduce it automatically? Misled by superficial analogies, didn't they perceive the differences which leapt to view? It is however obvious that the Russians, in spite of their admirable perseverance, would never have achieved "socialism in a single country" without the immense natural riches of Russia.[1] Cen-

---

[1] And without an almost inexhaustible man power.

tral Europe certainly does not lack resources but they are un-
equally distributed among the nations: socialist construction
necessitated the close union of all the Peoples Democracies
and the elaboration in common of plans of production. This
is what Nagy explained very clearly, as early as 1953, in his
speech to Parliament: "Nothing," he said, "justifies exaggerated industrialization; and this effort to achieve national industrial self-sufficiency, particularly if one does not have the
necessary resources in raw materials, constitutes a renouncing
of advantageous possibilities resulting from a more intensive
international exchange of merchandise and above all of economic collaboration with the U.S.S.R., the Peoples Democracies and Peoples China. It will be necessary to place the
accent on light industry and food processing while diminishing
considerably the rhythm of the development of heavy industry." By this he did not mean to denounce, as has been
thought, the primacy of heavy industry, any more than the
present collapse of the Hungarian and Polish economies necessarily puts this principle in question. What the Russians call
"the priority of increasing the production of the means of production" is a necessity which is also found in a capitalist economy since technical progress comes down, in the final analysis,
to the growing preponderance of the machine in the manufac-
ture of products. But this necessity—except in the case of
certain particularly favored powers—has above all as a consequence in the West, to reinforce the ties of dependency among
the nations and to push toward the constitution of cartels,
complexes, and international pools. The search for profit calls
all the shots, of course, but, in the present phase of industrial
development, the unification of complimentary economies is
a task which imposes itself everywhere, whatever the regime.
And Nagy doesn't mean anything else: for him, the priority of

heavy industry can be made firm within an organic whole where the resources of the soil and sub-soil sustain and satisfy the requirements of industrialization. One of his close collaborators is still more explicit: "We were mistaken because we wrongly interpreted the policy of socialist industrialization." The development of light industry, such as was attempted from 1953 to 1955 by the Nagy Government, did not mean the abandonment of the "Marxist-Leninist" thesis: they were only putting the accent on the impossibility of achieving in Hungary "socialism in a single country." The incredible folly of Stalin and the Stalinists was to believe in or to permit the belief in a pre-established harmony: actually, how can one explain, if not through a recourse to Providence, that each Peoples Democracy happened to be at the same time a complex product of universal history and an economic organism harboring within itself all or almost all the conditions for its autonomy? By what aberration was one persuaded that each of the Peoples Democracies had the duty of pushing industrialization to the limit in order to base its sovereignty on a true national self-sufficiency? And who then could delude himself that the sweat and blood of the workers would bring fertility to the land and call up coal or iron in the very places where they didn't exist?

In the beginning, no one supported this idiotic doctrine: as early as 1945, on the contrary, certain States of Central Europe had launched the idea of an economic federation. One can guess that Stalin did not look on it kindly: it seems nevertheless that he was not altogether against it; Tito had strange conversations with him on this subject. In fact, the fiercest resistance came from the small Balkan powers, always jealous of their autonomy, but it goes without saying that the federation—with or without them—would have been set up if only the Kremlin had decided so. In any case, the Marshall provocation destroys the feeble chances of federalism with one blow. The fixed habit of mistrust triumphs. It is not enough to tear these States away from the West's hold on them, it is necessary to isolate them, to divide in order to rule. "Socialism in a single country" had been the doctrine and the gigantic undertaking of a nation cut off from the world. In order to cut off from the surrounding world each Peoples Democracy, the latter was given for catechism and task "socialism in a single country." Stalinism keeps on exploiting the political enmities of the satellites. In order to hide from them that, in certain sectors, at least, their economies would be able to become complementary, they are forced to provide themselves artificially with homologous economies. With the assistance of the U.S.S.R.— experts, markets, material aid in emergencies—each will throw itself into superindustrialization and into the accelerated collectivization of the agricultural sector. This sudden frenzy was to have another effect: it was certainly expected that these populations, absorbed in an immense constructive work, would forget Marshall and his works; socialization Russian style was their proud response to the offers from abroad: we don't need anyone, we work for our own living. The U.S.S.R. was the mentor, it was guiding its younger sisters towards abundance: its solicitude would cause to be forgotten the meagerness of its material aid. In each Peoples Democracy, the leaders "laid it on thick": it was necessary to mask the Soviet dictatorship by exalting chauvinism; there was insistence on the admirable effort of the people who were winning independence by the sweat of their brows, there was the effort to give them tangible symbols of their victories: Rakosi has a subway constructed in Budapest despite the advice of experts: he erects Stalinvaros, an extraordinary dead city, an enormous building site where no one works; the Polish Stalinists want to endow the country with an automobile industry. In a word, there is an effort to base a new nationalism on the grandeur of the "achievements." Entirely cut off from its neighbors, each country adopts the retractile structure of Soviet society, it masks its subjugation and its misery by building a gigantic false front.

The goal was attained rapidly: the Governments sent each other telegrams, they were able to make courtesy visits, the nations could exchange delegations but the true relationships between Prague and Warsaw, between Belgrade and Budapest necessarily passed by way of Moscow; one finds again the principle of the Stalinist hierarchy: subordinates communicate with each other only through the intermediary of their superior. This was Stalin's fundamental error: rather than attaching its allies to it by a real and positive solidarity, the U.S.S.R. preferred to create monsters which could not exist without it.

In the very moment when nationalism was being exalted, the Stalinist distrust was busy humiliating it. No one seemed to take notice, indeed, of the unbridgeable gap which separated these prefabricated revolutions from the October Revolution. The latter was an autochthonal product. Whatever its later contradictions and the hierarchical society which they engendered, it came from below, it was borne by the masses, at least in the beginning. For the Peoples Democracies, on the contrary, socialism was an imported product, the Revolution had been made from on high, its chiefs had been imposed by the Red Army and many of them were back from Moscow. The only government which enjoyed popular confidence, Tito's, drew strength from the support of the masses to resist the demands of the U.S.S.R. The result is known: Stalinist distrust, reinforced, required the liquidation of "national Communists" everywhere else; now they were the only ones who had fought in the Resistance, the only ones who had kept some personal influence over the workers. The men who remained, as devoted as they were to socialism, owed their power only to support from abroad. I have told how the Soviet bureaucracy had cut itself off from the masses. But I have also shown that this break was the consequence of inevitable contradictions and extreme dangers. In the Peoples Democracies, the brutal dissolution of the Fronts and the Stalinization of the Communist Parties carried out this break *in advance* and threw discredit on the new policy when there had not yet been time to get ready for it. These Governments, born of the cold war, thought it wise to exalt nationalism in words, when their very existence was humiliating it in fact; they didn't understand that they were forming an army which would turn against them sooner or later. Rakosi pushed blindness even further: Jewish, surrounded by Jews, he did not fear reawakening the Hungarians' anti-semitism by a violent anti-Zionist campaign.

Everything tended toward abstraction: Merleau-Ponty is right to point out, in this connection, the failure of "voluntarist" economic planning which ends up in "unreal" projects. But he is wrong to extend this condemnation to the plans made for the U.S.S.R., by Soviet experts, the best informed on the requirements and possibilities of their national economy. Certainly, the anticipated results have not always been attained but these projects, however authoritarian and "voluntarist," with the margin of error which they can entail, remain valid or at least correctable as long as they are *national*. In the Peoples Democracies, the plans, elaborated by Russian experts, took no account of the real conditions of production; once set, no one could bring them back into question. Now these plans were only dreams: of course, they were requiring *too much* and *too fast*, but above all they asked for *something else*. Something else than that which could be given them. They imposed an artificial economy on the country which the real economy could not bear. To maintain these alien structures by force, each day more of the national income was drawn off: in Hungary, in the course of the execution of the Plan, between 1951 and 1953, the proportion of investments in heavy industry (added to the expenditures of State organism and to those of the administrative apparatus) did not cease to grow: fixed at first at 28 percent, two years later half of the income was swallowed up in it. Better yet, when the Soviet requirements varied they instituted, to satisfy them, a partial redistribution of investments, without ever reconsidering the entire economic planning: as a result, some sectors atrophied suddenly and others were getting hypertrophic; ulcers were eating away the economies.

The consequences are known by everyone; the hostility of the rural inhabitants wrecked the cooperatives everywhere; the Governments were not sure enough of their troops to have recourse to force. The fact is that the visible presence of the occupant was poisoning everything: Would Hungarian soldiers have fired on Hungarian peasants to force them to follow directives from abroad? Could one have recourse to Russian troops without aggravating the situation? The real power of the dictators was less solid than it seemed at first: they could hang bureaucrats but they were not succeeding in rallying the peasants nor even in freezing the workers on the job. Besides, the farmers knew the tragic history of the Soviet collectivization: one can be sure that the prewar bourgeois or fascist press had obligingly informed them; they were not trying to oppose by force the establishment of the cooperatives: but their passive resistance led to the ruin of the system. The standard of living remained stationary when it wasn't going down; in numerous industrial sectors, in spite of the tremendous effort which was imposed on the workers, productivity never caught up with the prewar level. The goals set by the Plan were attained only on paper. Each Peoples Democracy was double: there was the mirage society and the real society. The mirage society was the U.S.S.R. on a smaller scale: a bureaucracy drunk with statistics was, with an iron hand, leading the workers towards socialism; from top to bottom, the hierarchical order squeezed somewhat but kept individuals in place. The real society was the whirling about of an economy and a bureaucracy which had altogether lost their bearings, and then empty space, and then, on the level of the masses, an extraordinary mixture of constraint and anarchy.[1] The system was still holding up because no one knew the entire truth: the workers and technicians saw the gravity of the errors committed in their section but they couldn't conceive that it was the same in all the other sectors. The leaders didn't take the measure of the extent of the disasters: people lied to them, they lied to Stalin. Stalin and the Politburo stubbornly persisted in error: the characteristic of pessimism is to be corroborated by its effects. After the Marshall operation, the Soviet leaders had judged war more probable than peace. The logical consequence of this evaluation was rearmament, it was also the politics of blocs: in this perspective, which fed distrust, it was natural to treat as suspect these strange allies who had been in a hurry, in 1948, to lend their ear to the too beautiful sirens

---

[1] The poverty is such that many people do "moonlighting," that is to say, they take on one and sometimes two supplementary jobs. The result of this is that the real economy (partially based on clandestine work) is, in its very structure, different from a state-run economy. It must be said that the novelist Doudinzev points out the same fact in Moscow: insufficiently paid workers form a clandestine cooperative.

of the Atlantic. It has been said that the U.S.S.R. had *colonized* the satellite countries: this is wrong; colonization is a well-defined economic system whose characteristics are not found here: where has one seen colonizers force the colonized to become industrialized? The mother country exports finished products in order to import raw materials or food stuffs; now, between the U.S.S.R. and the Peoples Democracies the nature of the exchanges is eminently variable: Russia can buy mined products and pay for them with cereals (Polish coal for Soviet wheat); it can develop (in Czechoslovakia and even in Hungary) industries complementary to its own: it happens in this case that it delivers raw materials against its importations, that is to say, it plays the role of an underdeveloped country.[1] In other cases the exchange is a matter of manufactured objects. Without a doubt, people will say, but there is *exploitation*. That's not true either. Or, at least, it is not the main point. Certainly, the Soviet leaders have always sought to achieve agreements which would be advantageous to them. They have unceremoniously laid hands on Hungarian uranium; when they created joint companies, they arranged matters so that the computation of proportional returns assured them a supplementary margin of profit; it isn't to be doubted either that they were buying Polish coal below price. But, there again, the question has been exaggerated or badly put: what many Communists reproached the Russians for, in the Peoples Dem-

---

[1] Fejtö quite correctly notes: "Contrary to what characterizes in general the relations between highly industrialized powers and colonial or semi-colonial countries, which serve them as sources of cheap raw materials—here (in Hungary) a relatively underdeveloped great power found itself in a dominant position, confronting a country whose industrial capacity could fill out its own. The weakness of the U.S.S.R. compared to its economic and military needs thus explains that it did not prevent Hungary from developing its heavy industry, that on the contrary it pushed it too much in this direction. . . ." (*La Tragédie hongroise*, p. 108.)

ocracies, is not for buying below world prices (although that can have happened) but, quite to the contrary, for taking world prices as the basis of their calculations, which has the immediate result of disadvantaging the underdeveloped nation. In short these socialists were reproached for acting *like capitalists* and not for indulging in some sort of superexploitation which would make the capitalists themselves blush. In any case, it is not that which ruined the economies of the satellites; and one must not forget that this partial exploitation is compensated for in emergencies by a material aid. No, the U.S.S.R. did not colonize nor systematically exploit the Peoples Democracies. What is true is that it *oppressed* them for eight years. It could try to win their friendship and, deliberately, through pessimism and distrust, it preferred constraint. This big, solitary country couldn't and wouldn't break its shell of routine and distrust to adapt itself to the new situation and to assume the "leadership" of Central Europe. I have said distrust pays a price: oppressed, ruined, treated as suspect, these allies became less and less reliable. Force is its own Q.E.D.; in 1948 they bet on it; it is it alone, today, which guarantees the fidelity of Hungary to the Russians.

In Stalin's time, however, the sores remained covered over. No one can doubt that the events in Poland and Hungary were the direct result of what is here called *de-Stalinization*. De-Stalinization, democratization: whatever name it is given, this extraordinary upheaval doesn't come from the pressure of the masses. Nor from the intervention of the army. The Stalinist regime, from its birth, ceaselessly destroyed itself to the precise extent that, in comformity with its role, it was building an entirely different society from that which had produced it: in Stalin's last years, Stalinism had forged all the instruments for its liquidation. It was a relict, in profound contradiction with the real structure of the new society. The U.S.S.R. had acquired an enormous military potential: the Red Army was strong enough to reach the Atlantic in forty-eight hours; the armament industry was making atomic bombs. It wasn't sure that the Russians would win in a world conflict, but it already appeared that one could not attack them without putting the human race on the brink of total disappearance. In the same time—and *in spite of* Stalin's systematic distrust—a great Communist power had just been born, which had made its revolution itself, without help, and which—contrary to the Peoples Democracies—indissolubly united, from the beginning, the requirements of socialist construction with those of the national interest:[1] Mao's China kept the U.S.S.R. safe from encirclement. It is an understatement to say, as has been said, that these new conditions permitted a policy of détente: they demanded it. Alone and hunted down, vulnerable, the U.S.S.R. could show itself violent without ceasing to affirm its desire for peace: the relationship of forces was unfavorable to it; the intransigence of its diplomacy and, if I may say so, its aggressiveness remained defensive. Its relative inferiority placed it in the necessity of rejecting—at least in appearance—all concessions. This negative attitude corresponded perfectly to the Stalinist "pull back." But when Stalin had announced that the Soviet industry was making nuclear weapons, when Mao had proclaimed the Chinese Republic, this "retractile" attitude became more and more dangerous: the relationship of forces tending to balance out, the Stalinist aggressiveness was changing its direction in spite of itself and becoming objectively offensive. The Korean war was the test: it is clear that the U.S.S.R. is not responsible for it and that these local operations represent an episode of the conflict—quite serious in

---

[1] How many overseas Chinese rallied to Peoples China from *nationalism!*

other respects—which was then setting Peoples China against the America of MacArthur and of the "China lobby."[1] But the American Government judged otherwise. One knows by what press campaigns the public was panicked and how anti-Sovietism was aggravated. In any case, the "awakening" of the U.S.A., the hardening of its policy, McCarthyism and the decision to rearm Germany testify to a sudden panic: the U.S.S.R. becoming strong enough to reveal its imperialism, the war clan took on increasing importance in the U.S.A. The Kremlin had to resign itself to war or take an attitude more in keeping with its new and terrible power. At the same time, moreover, the triumph of the Chinese Communists was pulling the U.S.S.R. out of its isolation but, as a counterpart, it was summoning it to establish, *with one country at least*, true socialist relationships. There could be no question of subjugating and making a fief of a nation of six hundred million inhabitants; however, China was underdeveloped, the gap between the two economies was such that it threatened to lead the Soviets down the path of semi-colonialism: it was necessary to choose between an exploitation, even discreet, which the Chinese economy could not have borne, and the truly socialist practice of disinterested aid. Only this policy of giving permitted the U.S.S.R. to preserve its hegemony over the socialist world;

---

[1] The aggression comes from North Korea, the provocation from Syngman Rhee, the ultimate responsibility falls totally on MacArthur. He did everything to catch China in the Korean trap. I remind the abstract visionaries, who consider the world a chess board and who imagine Stalin in the process of seizing the North Korean pawn in order to put it down brutally on the "South Korean" square, that the North Koreans condemned to death and shot those of their leaders who were in power when the conflict broke out. In the face of the *fait accompli*, China and the U.S.S.R. could not react alike: the former could not compromise its young prestige by letting an Asiatic people be crushed at its gates, it knew at its own cost that Korea was and can still be the classic route of Japanese invasions; the latter found itself cornered: it had to stand back at the risk of a world war or alienate Asia by a clumsy interventionism.

still it must be added that this hegemony, in China, was to remain very limited; the Soviet leaders were not unaware of it: it was through China and through it alone that they could exercise their influence over the Asiatic world but the prestige of the Chinese Republic remained inseparable from its independence and its sovereignty. From 1949 on, the U.S.S.R. found itself constrained, for the first time, to base its relations with a foreign nation on confidence and generosity.[1]

Meanwhile, the structure of Soviet society had not ceased to evolve. Economic blockade was no longer to be feared, the U.S.S.R. had become the second industrial power of the world. The primacy accorded to heavy industry and armaments had put a brake on the rise of the standard of living but had not stopped it. This rise attenuated the fundamental contradiction between the requirements of industrialization and the needs of the worker. The level of culture had considerably risen: educated, knowing, the young workers no longer had anything in common with the illiterate masses of 1926; they could foresee and give their assistance to rational and clearly explained economic planning; on the other hand they were finding it difficult to put up with the authoritarianism of petty Stalins in the factories or shops, and still more difficult to put up with the existence of a Stakhanovite elite whose interests opposed theirs. The new rural generation had not known prewar massacres and deportations; it was beginning, moreover, to feel the benefits of motorization: this is what was bringing it, little by little, closer to the regime. At the head of the manufacturing plants and the State technical research centers a generation of technicians, tough and ambitious but solidly trained, were rediscovering *in work* open relationships with the peasants and workers. People have talked of "technocracy": this is absurd.

---

[1] What followed is well-known (1964).

But there's no doubt that the second phase of socialist construction is characterized by the growing importance of technology and that the specialists therein are protected and valued for their functions. This new importance in direct liaison with productivity tends to shield them from Stalinism: their consecration comes from their capacities; it is the latter which protects them from the risks of disgrace and which is at the base in each one of the consciousness he has of himself.

However, at the top, the dictatorship was becoming unnerved; terror was running wild, spinning faster and faster, destroying everything; the isolation of the Party was being accentuated; from the top to the bottom of the social ladder an incompetent bureaucracy duplicated the new technical cadres. This bureaucracy had had its heroic hour: when cadres were lacking, it had learned everything by itself, it had hastily acquired culture and the technical knowledge which permitted it, for better or for worse, to direct the industrialization. Stalin was the model of these great workers: he read everything, was acquainted with everything, decided on everything, he found time to have all films shown to him, to judge all novels, all musical compositions; the necessities of his office had obliged him to acquire what one could call, with a mixture of censure and admiration, a universal incompetence. But to the very extent that these bureaucrats *stood in place of* experts and specialists, to the extent that they bridged the gap between ignorant Tsarist Russia and industrialized U.S.S.R., they were digging their own grave: higher education, created and developed thanks to them, was producing ever more numerous technicians, whose role was precisely to eliminate them. They were still on deck, however, these Stalinists who owed all to Stalin: the bureaucracy allied to the Party distrusted newcomers and believed itself to be the sole depository of revolutionary élan: this meant, above all, that it judged itself alone qualified to establish plans and to assure their execution. Thus, in the last years of Stalin, the movement of socialization was engendering a latent contradiction, which the dictatorship still masked but which was to break out sooner or later: by producing its new cadres, it was setting them against the old ones.[1] There were two regimes in the U.S.S.R.: on one side a too strong hierarchical society where the inequalities remained flagrant, but which had provided itself, under Stalin and thanks to Stalinism, with its own institutions, structure and coherence; in spite of its internal contradictions, this society *stood by itself*, it was evolving without cease but its bases were solid, it was protected against violent breakdowns or atomization by its internal organs of coordination and mediation; the capability of its cadres and the extent of capital equipment made it possible for it to *carry* the Plan, to sustain it instead of being dragged along by it: ultimately the Plan was to merge with the concrete movement of production; on the other side, a police dictatorship without real utility and an administration incapable of resolving new problems, of overcoming contradictions or of arbitrating conflicts. Even the di-

---

[1] One of the first results of de-Stalinization will be the liquidation of the old myth "bourgeois science and proletarian science." This means that this builders' society wants to shield its scientists from the absurd influence of the bureaucracy. It is not a question of re-establishing science "in its eminent dignity," as is said in our country, but of putting it entirely at the service of technology. "The blundering interference of incompetent persons has made us lose too much time," a Russian told me.

One will also note in many novels published in recent years the almost classical opposition between the administrator and the scientist or engineer. Naturally, the administrator is an arrivist who does not have the confidence of the workers and who knows very little outside of his political catechism; the engineer on the contrary, is a useful and real man because he deals with material objects and machines; because of that, he is the workers' friend. This tie (more or less close) between worker and technician against the bureaucrat is clearly indicated, for example, in the first part of *The Thaw*.

recting bureaucracy could no longer tolerate the terror which it had engendered and maintained: destruction by forces from without was no more to be feared than counterrevolution from within: no one any longer completely believed in the pagan idol of Absolute Unity; distrust had engendered this cult, the cult would disappear with the distrust: the relaxing of the dictatorship would carry with it the return to collective leadership whose flexible unity is based on the reciprocity of relationships. The new organizers, collaborators and subordinates of Stalin, lived in contradiction: they belonged simultaneously to a terrible but inefficient system which no longer had any other reality than that of the blood it shed and to a society of technicians, of workers whose concrete relations depended above all on the mode of production and who required a government of managers and arbiters.

Dangerous in foreign policy, the system, on the domestic scene, could only slow down the development of production. Stalinism was a relict the only reason for which is to be sought in the very existence of Stalin. As long as he remained, above all others, as the symbol of a necessary dictatorship, the new Soviet society did not have the means to come to know itself: the policy of blocs was keeping the cold war alive and, with it, the vague feeling that a terrible threat weighed on the U.S.S.R. —the same one, exactly, which had obscured the horizon since 1917; and then there was the slogan "the class struggle becomes intensified when socialism is neared" which justified all appeals for "vigilance," there was the propaganda which was hard at work raising everywhere the specter of the hidden enemy. The system was fed, sustained by Stalin and Stalin, grown old, was the first victim of the system: raised to power by universal distrust, he remained the incarnation of this distrust when it no longer had a *raison d'être*; to the very extent that he sensed the divergence between his own system and the society which he had forged, he could no longer react except by accentuating his distrust. For having been the instigator and the agent of the "pull back" which had allowed the U.S.S.R. to win the war, he had rendered himself completely incapable of directing the Soviet expansion. A man is made by his praxis: it transforms him, it discovers its principles through him, and, when it no longer has a grip on reality, it withdraws within him and settles in his brain, in his muscles, in the form of sheer habit. From 1948 on, the new terror was routine. The "plot of the doctors" had an air of *"déjà vu,"* an anachronistic appearance which increased its horror; heads rolled but the real structure of society was not changed. The contrast between the old rancid pessimism of the Stalinists and the optimism of the builders became more pronounced each day; this young society, rightly proud of its successes, was cut off from itself by a bloody and chaotic nightmare.

The principal factor of the de-Stalinization, one is forced to admit, is quite simply the death of Stalin: a funeral veil slips aside, revealing Soviet society to its own eyes. An outworn conception of social integration disappears at the same time as the only man capable of imposing it. That is exactly what makes the return of a dictator impossible: the collectivity would no longer recognize itself in him; the elements of this social body, welded together by multiple integrations—vertical and horizontal—are achieving unity through a complex plurality of hierarchies and of reciprocity: they neither need unification *from on high* nor the romantic myth of incarnate unity. It was necessary *to be Stalin already* to prolong for some time a useless dictatorship, but his successors, even if they wanted to, would not have the means to imitate him: they are not sacred, they can not become so: this positive society liquidated idols and cults. One has read a hundred times in the bourgeois press that Malenkov, Khrushchev, Molotov and the others "squabbled over Stalin's succession." This is absurd. After the death of an emperor, Roman generals could contend for his throne: the imperial power did not depend on the man who was temporarily exercising it. But how could one vie for Stalin's succession *since it doesn't exist.* Stalin left nothing behind him except a world which he made and which repudiates him. De-Stalinization, originally, was a discovery rather than a decision: freed from the great Stalinist shadow, the leaders simultaneously lost omnipotence and subservience; they would remain, no matter what they did, plunged in national collectivity and no one could any longer rise above it. The "retractile" policy became impossible; it was necessary to perfect a policy of expansion: how to give life back to the bureaucracy, to the Party, to these two organs bleeding and shriveled up from the Stalinist domination, without having them first recover the confidence of the masses? But how would the masses give them their confidence if first of all the Party didn't give them its own, in short, if a certain control of the base over the apparatus were not re-established? Stakhanovism had been born from distrust, constraint and scarcity: it provoked hostility, a passive resistance among most workers. To raise productivity, the masses had to become interested in it; and how to interest them without first of all *giving* to them? A redistribution of investments would bring the moment closer when they would be conscious of working for themselves by working for the nation. In a word, the only policy *possible* must be entirely positive, base itself on optimism and confidence. The U.S.S.R. of Stalin had distrusted others because it had no confidence in itself; the new Russia was changing policy because it was finally discovering that it could have confidence in itself; now, it was strong enough, in all domains, to open its doors proudly to the West. For a young country, sure of its strength, you don't always count on the worst; it can bet on peace: the new policy was to develop on all planes at the same time; it would succeed only in a climate of international détente, but it would contribute to creating this climate. It didn't go very far, as is known, along the paths of democracy—and besides democratization as such was the least concern of the leaders—nor did it seek to get rid of the most flagrant inequalities, to combat poverty efficiently: but it was, with all its inadequacies, the only true policy because it was in accord with the movement which involved the whole nation, with the constant raising of its industrial and military potential, with the hope, with the ardent desire to live of the new generations, a simple subjective expression of these extraordinary transformations. And it doesn't help anything to repeat that the de-Stalinizers are Stalinists. What else could they be? This curious argument reminds me of that of the Girondins who reproached Robespierre with having been, like them, a Royalist before August 10th. So what? It is with the Royalists that the French Revolution made the Republic and Republicans; it is de-Stalinization which will de-Stalinize the de-Stalinizers. For the changes already started cannot stop there: this society, in discovering itself, discovers also its conflicts and its weak spots. The working class is formed of new men who have acquired awareness of their powers and their rights; it is true that they have, in return, lost the traditions of revolutionary struggle: but, to keep things straight, one must recognize that it is not a question of making the Revolution; within a society which is founded on the socialization of the means of production, the working class can and must obtain profound reforms but the Revolution is *be-*

hind it.[1] This class, as soon as terror ends, can no longer avoid seeing its contradictions: they were concealed from it in the name of Public Welfare but the danger is getting more remote, it sees that its practical condition is in opposition to its theoretical role as dictatorial class, it is subject to an economic planning which it ought to contribute to establishing. Its culture—by far superior to that of any other proletariat—permits it to see clearly; it will clearly formulate its problems and its requirements. Thus the movement which is started within the Soviet Society can be only a return to the sources of socialism: the increase in productivity requires at present that one have confidence in the masses; and the latter, after having *received* culture more than they have *conquered* it, must find again their proper activity and emancipate themselves through reformist combat. De-Stalinization is a policy of victory, based on the continual growth of a giant nation and which must sooner or later, willy-nilly, free all the positive forces of this society. It rejects Stalinist pessimism under its pseudo-Marxist form—it is not true that the construction of socialism intensifies class struggle—and substitutes its own principles for it: you don't always count on the worst and man is not always evil; one must prepare for peace by peace. In truth, it matters little that the de-Stalinizers have not entirely freed themselves from Stalinism: what can be disquieting, is that there remains in the upper and middle cadres a considerable quantity of bureaucrats whose interests are opposed to de-Stalinization. It is not a question, as has been claimed, of the interests of a class, not even of a milieu: the Stalinists are recruited just about every-

---

[1] This doesn't mean that there cannot be here and there—as in Poznan or Budapest—bloody insurrections, but quite simply that the bureaucracy and the new technical administration are not classes.

where and their interests are indistinguishable from those of the bureaucracy *qua* organ of government: each of them risks being dethroned by a specialist as the universal machine was dethroned by specialized machines. To the very extent that the technician represents the pure and simple expression of objectivity, he tends to bring out the inefficiency of an authoritarian decision which would not be based on the course of things. To the extent that the preponderance of machinery becomes more pronounced in the composition of manufactured products, economic planning passes out of the hands of the bureaucrats-Stalinists: the rate of increase in productivity no longer depends so much on men and on the constraint exercised over them; it is bound up more each day with the improvements of techniques and with the perfectioning of machines. It is equipment itself, one might say, which through the mediation of engineers, defines its own possibilities and, in conjunction with the necessity of interesting all of the masses in production, determines investment policy. Confronted by these new requirements, the incumbents risk discovering their uselessness. They defend themselves by identifying their cause with that of the Revolution: many of them are sincere, one could not deny it; they have always conceived of the revolutionary movement as a fierce effort, imposed on all by constraint and sustained by the heroism of the best of them: the rough hewn peasant who joined the industrial proletariat, around 1930, had to be wrenched out of himself, pushed to the limit of his strength; the whole society, under the impulsion of the bureaucrats and the Party, constantly was in process of outdoing itself, *more* was asked of it than it could give: no one is unaware that the objectives of the first five-year plans were not attained. This wrenching process justified Stalinist pessimism and kept it from turning into complete misanthropy: human nature was merely weakness, egoism, its needs impeded economic planning, but the Stakhanovite was the true Stalinist hero because he rejected his nature and because he represented, in sum, the negation of a negation. In this perspective, one can imagine that the administration and the organs of the State do not view without concern the development of a society which each day is becoming more technical: where will revolutionary impetus come from? If the masses absorb the heroes of labor, if technicians control production, won't the movement of socialization slow down? Won't the permanent tension of the collectivity slacken? Isn't there the danger of promoting the stratification of social layers? It is very significant that Stalin, shortly before his death, had the chairman of the five-year Plan shot, accusing him of wanting to re-establish capitalism: this was the brutal reaction of the revolutionary bureaucrat against the technician. Of course, this concern is idle: it simply shows that the Party is necessary for the building of socialism and that it must preserve its function as agitator and pace-setter of men *on the express condition* of changing its structure. But the Stalinists of the apparatus cannot even conceive of this metamorphosis; they have only one concern: to take these new generations in hand. Khrushchev worries about the youth: just the other week he issued a severe warning to the students, that is to say, to the future technicians. Molotov tries to intimidate the painters and writers. I am not saying that one or the other is the representative of Stalinist bureaucrats: it is up to the super-lucid to decide that.[1] What is certain, is that they both reflect the current contradictions of Soviet society and that they are together undergoing contrary influences according to the moment and the conjuncture of circumstances. What can be disturbing is

---

[1] We now know what it was all about (1964).

that the existence of these Stalinist elements, still numerous and powerful, both conservative and revolutionary, engenders and maintains, without as well as within, a dangerous illusion: it would seem, in fact, that the Soviet bureaucracy has at its disposal a substitute policy and a substitute team all ready to carry it out. This is wrong: the team exists perhaps but not the policy: "neo-Stalinism" is not viable, it was born headless; what is called by this name is the desperate effort of a group to defend its privileges and its prejudices. Where can this lead? To its liquidation, if we are lucky. If not, to disordered convulsions, error, crime, war.

Unfortunately, each time that the West bets on the worst, it increases the influence in the East of those who have bet on war. All clear-sighted men, whatever their political tendency, have said and repeated that response should have been made to the first overtures from the U.S.S.R.; all have shown that great risks would be taken in discouraging the nascent de-Stalinization. Unfortunately, in our country also the cold war changed the structure of society; everywhere, anticommunism brought conservatives to power: they are the natural allies of Stalinism; and then there are the armaments manufacturers: the specter of peace plunged them into panicky terror. Anything, but not *that*: their representatives hastened to vote for the rearmament of Germany. Ruinous, ineffective, this rearmament had only one advantage: it blocked de-Stalinization, it re-established the cold war. Sure enough, Khrushchev replaced Malenkov and reaffirmed the primacy of heavy industry.

But what, from the very beginning, tipped the scales in favor of the Stalinists was the insurrectional strike in Berlin. The Soviet leaders learned two disagreeable truths at once: the Governments of the allied countries had lied to them, the situation of the satellites was very different from the picture they had drawn of it: de-Stalinization was not a specifically Soviet phenomenon; it was necessarily to spread to the Peoples Democracies and its repercussions would be all the more serious since the economies were more unbalanced. In the U.S.S.R., victory was being de-Stalinized: the regime was stable, accepted by all, industry powerful, production maintained and could increase its rate of growth, the standard of living, still very low, was continually rising. In the satellite countries defeat was being de-Stalinized: if the restraint was loosened, they would discover crimes, ruinous errors, wasted resources, a handful of isolated Stalinists confronting hostile populations who detested their Government, the Russians, and perhaps socialism. No more than Stalinism was de-Stalinization an export commodity: in Central Europe, the Soviet de-Stalinizers were finding themselves making common cause with the creatures of Stalin. Malenkov had facilitated Nagy's return to power, Khrushchev replaced him with Rakosi. But the new policy was developing by itself, in the U.S.S.R. and abroad: the general movement of expansion obliged the Russians to settle their dispute with Tito. And how could they succeed in that without proclaiming that socialism can be achieved by different paths, that is to say, without encouraging *in all the Peoples Democracies* these "national Communists" whose chiefs had been executed or imprisoned? The public prosecutors had, at the time, tried above all to bring Tito to trial; now, Tito, the winner, was demanding that all verdicts be annulled. The profound contradiction of this policy is obvious: the Soviet leaders were supporting the Stalinists of Central Europe but they were discrediting them by reconciling themselves with the Yugoslavs. Khrushchev and Bulganin had an easy time of it throwing on Beria and on Stalin the lies and crimes of 1950 by adding discreetly: "*We* were not yet in power." But in Central Europe, those whom Stalin had compromised, those whom he had constrained to become his accomplices, were in power in 1950 and they were still there in 1955: if Rajk was innocent, a martyr, the head of the Hungarian Government turned out to be an assassin. Rakosi did not seem sensitive to this pitiless logic; unfortunately for him, the logic had imposed itself on the entire Hungarian people. The Russians had brought back the dictators in the Red Army's vehicles: they had made them suspect by installing them in power, detestable by forcing them to make terror reign; now, they were dishonoring them by obliging them to proclaim their crimes and to kiss Tito's feet. All this would not have been very serious if these criminals, right after their confessions, had been hanged. But where was the substitute team to be found? It existed: in the prisons there were men with broken teeth, with fingernails torn out, who had kept the sympathy of the people. Having been imprisoned on Stalin's order, the Soviet Government doubted that they could become faithful allies: this was undoubtedly its greatest error: the old Stalinist distrust prevented it from understanding that these sincere Communists would put the interest of socialism and their own country before their personal resentments and that they would renew—on different bases—their alliance with Russia. And from where did this distrust come, it will be asked? Were the "Stalinists" regaining lost territory? Maybe: Tito has made sure that we know that the struggle was hot between the old bureaucracy and the representative of the new technical administration. But what counted above all is that the de-Stalinizers, vis-a-vis the Peoples Democracies, never abandoned Stalin's attitude: they didn't trust them, they were nests of fascists, of ignoramuses, of cretins, of camouflaged bourgeois;[1] the workers were only Social-Democrats. The disastrous consequences of the economic planning furnished them with an additional proof: it was the peoples' fault. Thus the failure of the Stalinist policy invited them to keep it up.

The Twentieth Congress has a meaning which escapes us. It suffices to compare the official speech of Khrushchev with his famous secret report to understand that the latter was improvised, drawn up in haste; it has been compared to a kind of Shakespearian monologue, the apparent disorder of which dissimulates a visceral order and the reading of which tells nothing about Stalinism or the character of Stalin. Is it a personal initiative? Was it the Politburo which charged Khrushchev with drawing it up? We don't know. We don't know either whether the desire was to disarm the Stalinist opposition by overthrowing its idol or whether, by an unexpectedly high bid, it was an attempt to go beyond the timid efforts of the de-Stalinizers in order to regain the initiative and to put a brake on the de-Stalinization. In any case, this brutal maneuver was expressly destined for internal use: the reading of the report took place in the absence of foreign delegates; it was prudently distributed, with commentaries, in the factories and the kolkhozes; it seems that it was communicated only to the leaders of the satellite countries. The result is known, inevitable and perhaps sought: it was Polichinelle's secret; in the Peoples Dem-

---

[1] Here is, for example, a dialogue reported by Tito which took place between Stalin and him during 1944:

" 'Walter, look out! the bourgeoisie is very strong in Serbia!'

" 'Comrade Stalin . . . I don't agree with you on this point. The Serbian bourgeoisie is very weak.'

"He was silent, frowning, and the others around the table—Molotov, Zhdanov, Malenkov and Beria—were left open-mouthed."

Later—still from distrust, convinced of the bourgeois strength and the weakness of his own allies—Stalin tries to persuade Tito that it was necessary to restore King Peter.

ocracies, everyone, at the end of a week, was acquainted with it. Once again the consequences of de-Stalinization in the U.S.S.R. were to have their repercussions in Central Europe; and that, neither Khrushchev nor the Political Bureau had wanted: the blow was terrible; it broke the Communist Parties of the Peoples Democracies in two: the leaders and their accomplices realized that they must disappear or else impose themselves by force; but already force was slipping away from them: honest militants refused to support them. In Italy, Togliatti was denouncing the collective responsibility of the Soviet leaders: they had defended Stalin's policy or had made themselves its agents. If these accusations were not officially carried in the press of the "satellites," they had all the more impact when the Poles, the Hungarians, the Rumanians took responsibility for them within the Party, in the factories or in the universities. By an unjust but necessary reversal, the brutal frankness of the Russians made them lose their prestige. They were reproached both for having committed the faults which they were denouncing and for not explaining them. A contradictory reproach: by attaching these crimes to the very conditions of the socialization in the U.S.S.R., they would have partially cleared themselves of them. However, it was just for that that they could not be forgiven: by making Stalin a devil, they had replaced white masses with black masses and they had not at all gotten out of the cult of personality. The truth is that the operation was limited *for them and in the U.S.S.R.* to breaking up the idol; they did not intend at any price that the Soviet society could appear to the Russians as the monstrous product of a deviation. But for the allied countries who had suffered so much and who were discovering that they had been ruined, for the militants of Central Europe who had not invented the cult of Stalin and who had received it as a prefabricated product, the question of deviation was posed straightaway: weren't the satellites dragged into the orbit of a planet gone mad and off its axis? This time, the breakdown point had been reached: after Poznan, the Russians sensed that their allies were slipping from their grasp.

De-Stalinization is at the origin of the events of Poland, of Rumania and of Hungary; inversely, the U.S.S.R. had to suffer the backlash of the Central European disturbances: for never having abandoned their distrust, for having refused to envisage constructive solutions when it was necessary, the Soviet leaders ended up taking fright and having recourse to force. I don't know whether a "Stalinist faction" exists in the Politburo or whether this entire organism oscillates between two extreme positions and passes from one to the other according to circumstances. What is certain is that neo-Stalinism has triumphed. The neo-Stalinists doubtless do not approve of Stalin's crimes but they resemble him in that they commit the same ones "by necessity" and without perceiving that they are crimes. They are expecting the worst and are coming back to the idea that a world war is probable, perhaps certain, without understanding that the relationship of forces and of military potentials tends towards equilibrium, that we have never been further from universal conflagration and that it would be enough if they no longer feared it to make the specter disappear altogether. But in their formidable obstinacy, they resume the verbal violence which could be tolerated in the days when the U.S.S.R. was weaker, without perceiving that this verbal violence is totally intolerable today. When Bulganin threatens Paris and London with atomic rockets, he is not really thinking of using them; but these weapons exist, the U.S.S.R. possesses some, this is known; at once the threat takes on, from his lips, a reality which he perhaps does not realize. Has he even reflected for a moment that his bombs would burst on Saint-Denis, on Saint-Ouen, on Billancourt more often than on the roof of the Hôtel Matignon? These ill-considered remarks indirectly threatened the Parisian and London proletariats with death at the very moment when the Russian tanks were firing on the Hungarian proletariat; these remarks are only mutterings, one knows, but they seem to portend through their ominous carelessness the deliberate choice of barbarism and total chaos. It is known that it was necessary, for these words and for still others, to send apologies to Nehru.[1] The fact is there is only one way to avoid the

---

[1] Here is one of the most comic results of the neo-Stalinist contradiction. The bureaucratic leadership wants to practice the policy of pull back and of distrust without losing the positions which the policy of political expansion has won for it. As a result it becomes a Janus Bifrons. All went well when Nehru was only an agent of the U.S.A., a scoundrel: his protests couldn't touch Stalin since they *proved* that he was in the other camp. But when, from the point of view of a positive policy, the extreme importance of India and of the Hindu Government was recognized, when things were pushed so far as to pay a visit to its chief and to invite him to the U.S.S.R., when, from its direction, another great Communist power, China, considers him as a possible mediator between the Government of Washington and that of Peking, then it must be recognized that a certain control over Soviet policy has been conceded to this outside Minister, to this great outside nation. Let's not exaggerate: this control can only be exercised by speeches in India and by votes in the U.N. However, it is already formidable: Nehru's position allows him to influence opinion. Thus Stalinism *has no meaning* in regard to India: and the formal condemnation of the Soviet intervention has not resulted in breaking the friendship between the Russian and Hindu Governments. But at the same moment, the U.S.S.R. turns toward the West and makes threats—to divert attention from Hungary—though it renders its remarks harmless in a note addressed to Nehru. The result is, phrases with double meanings which are at the same time a verbal outburst of violence and simply noises, an objective reminder of Soviet strength and an uncontrolled reaction which limits itself to expressing the subjective temper of the leaders. For it is *on the grounds of subjectivity* that they excuse themselves: "We're a bit quick tempered, it's true, sometimes we say more than we should, but what do you expect, it's more than we can take: so much has been done to us!" It's one of the most curious characteristics of the new Stalinist diplomacy: the recourse to the subjective as a draw-back position. It is necessary for the policy of expansion: this is what allows

threatening war and to win it if, in spite of everything, it takes place: to get ready for it. One comes back, then, to the policy of blocs. Is it possible that the Soviet Government really thought that the pathetic Anglo-French attempt, that this flubbed landing could be the source of a world conflict? The whole world condemned us; in the U.N. our representatives were put in the corner with dunces' caps. It was enough for Messrs. Khrushchev and Shepilov to speak of their volunteers: we promised to be good. But this threat wasn't even necessary: a few ships sunk in the canal put us at the mercy of the U.S.A.; we would have sold our souls and the shreds which remained of our "military honor" for a few drops of gasoline. Now there is no doubt that the forces of war, today in America, are in clear retreat.[1] At a meeting of the Peace Movement, a deputy, as I have already mentioned, uttered these significant words: "How come you ask our Movement to concern itself

---

attenuating the numerous conflicts which can arise at the moment of first encounters. It's a sign of de-Stalinization: not because of the subjective turn—which doesn't have much to do with foreign policy—but *first of all* because it arises from a new situation in which *adaptation* is necessary. Stalin never got angry, he always kept the same cold and incisive tone: but it is because he was cut off from the world. Several great men *visited him*; he never visited anyone: it is hard to imagine him at a banquet in London offered by British Laborites.

[1] We will try in a coming issue [of *Les Temps Modernes:* TR.] to analyze the situation of the U.S.A. and to show the new social structures. But, for the moment, it suffices to recall that nuclear bombs became—in a certain measure—a factor for peace from the moment that the U.S.S.R. found out how to make them. There remain the classical risks of super-armament: but at the present time, they are less menacing. Certainly, the war industry has finally become a key sector of the American economy (as indeed of the Soviet economy) but the danger of crisis is temporarily more remote: technical inventions and improvements constantly renew the stock of arms and even prevent its formation. The military budget remains crushing: it is a favorable condition for negotiations on disarmament. The Korean war was a test for the American Government as for the Russian Government: the population showed itself hostile to it; Eisenhower got himself elected because he promised to stop the conflict. In case of an entente, the reconversion of the war industries is not impossible: it can express itself by aid granted on both sides to underdeveloped countries.

with the Hungarian events? It is not in Hungary that world peace is threatened: no one will go to war for Budapest. It's in the Middle East that the fire can break out." Translate: the West washes its hands of what is happening in Hungary; but the U.S.S.R. can consider the Franco-British aggression as a *casus belli*. Now, this intervention had abject but strictly limited goals: it was an effort *to keep,* not to conquer. Eden wished to protect the stockowners of the Company; Mollet, under Lacoste's influence, had conceived the stupid project of crushing, at Port Said, the "fellahs" of Algiers. To find in this miserable expedition, prepared without the knowledge of the U.S.A., the proof of a stiffening of the West, it is necessary to have bet already on war: what it reveals, to the contrary, are the contradictions of the bourgeois imperialism*s* and the conflicts of interests which are undermining the Atlantic Bloc. But already the U.S.S.R. panics: rockets on Paris! volunteers in Egypt! It reminds people that its troops can reach the Channel in forty-eight hours. Where is the smooth tone of Khrushchev saying to Guy Mollet: "Settle your business of Algeria. But *settle it quickly*: we won't give you any trouble"? In this pessimistic perspective, the failure of the Central European "Plans" disturbs neo-Stalinism less than social unrest: if the Hungarian economy is rickety, never mind that, it will be readjusted from on high, by an authoritarian move. But first of all the insurrection must be crushed. Not to save socialism in Hungary: but to save it in the U.S.S.R. Not for fear of the fascist émigrés, nor even of the Social-Democrats: because of the repercussions which a victory of the insurgents might have on the Rumanians, the Czechs, and above all the Germans. A success of the insurgents in Budapest and eastern Germany rises up; if the Red Army intervenes, Bonn's soldiers cross the line; it's world conflict. Neo-Stalinism fears or claims to fear that this conflict will originate in the Middle East but it is in Europe that it judges the situation explosive; for the Soviet leaders, it's in Europe that war will break out, engendered by the dislocation of their own bloc. Rather than run up against it with satellites in revolt, they strike; they don't mind destroying the chances of socialism in Hungary for fifty years as long as this bloody example paralyzes with terror the other "satellites."

People say that the Soviet leaders sought to save the world chance for socialism. I believe it. But true socialism is not separable from the real praxis of real men who are struggling together against the bosses, the cops, sometimes against the State and against its soldiers. And I am still too abstract: for it isn't even a movement; no, it is men on the march who group together and carry each other along, who organize themselves and change in organizing, who are made by history and who make it; their action is based on their needs and their needs are as true as themselves. But the socialism in the name of which Soviet soldiers fired on the masses in Hungary, I don't know, I cannot even conceive of it: it is not made for men nor by them; it is a name which is given to a new form of alienation. It has been claimed that the U.S.S.R. was defending its national interests in Budapest: this is both true and unjust. For the U.S.S.R., a socialist country, national interests are never distinguishable from the interests of socialism: likewise the Puritan of New England did not distinguish his own prosperity from Divine benediction and took up arms to defend at the same time God and private property. Only that does not condemn *all* Soviet policy; to the contrary: in a perspective of expansion, the aid furnished without counterpart to China and the underdeveloped countries establishes socialist relationships between the nations, and at the same time it enlarges the Russian zone of influence. But when the U.S.S.R. goes back to a

115

retractile policy, socialism and nationalism, inseparably, become *Reason of State*. It no longer is a question of saving men, workers' conquests, the concrete future of a socialization underway, but of preserving by force positions which, in the perspective of a world war, could advantage the Soviet nation, its armies and its armaments industry. And, of course, the U.S.S.R. must live, it is necessary *for the cause of communism*: all men of the Left will admit it. But it is also necessary that it remain socialist. One can no longer find in the Reason of State which it can invoke today anything but a vague reference to a future socialism; the concrete struggle of the masses is drowned in blood in the name of a pure abstraction which sets itself up as essential and which casts into insignificance and particularity all men of flesh and bones, be they workers, be they Communists. We are of those who say: the end justifies the means; but adding this indispensable corrective: it is the means which define the end. The U.S.S.R. is not imperialistic, the U.S.S.R. is peaceful, the U.S.S.R. is socialist: that's right. But when its leaders, in order to save socialism, send the army of the people against an allied country, when they have their soldiers fire on these abstract beings, on workers who can no longer bear their misery, when, without taking into consideration the concrete requirements of the situation, they decide on their action in terms of the repercussions it can have *elsewhere,* on other countries, and, finally on the world, they make of socialism a chimera and transform the U.S.S.R., in spite of them, in spite of it, into a predatory nation. The workers of all countries have too often served as a target for soldiers to accept, wherever it be and whatever the reason invoked, that regular troops massacre the people: the Soviet armored vehicles, in Budapest, fired in the name of socialism on all the proletariats of the world. Now, if socialism does not determine the nature of the undertakings which claim to safeguard it: if one believes one can protect it by methods which are allied to the Tsarist repressions, it becomes an indifferent and passive object, an ideal term of reference which one can replace, anywhere and any time, by an abstraction. The leaders know it since they lie to their people: this is to admit clearly that they refuse to count on the approval of the Soviet workers and that they behaved like authoritarian bureaucrats rather than like elected representatives of the nation: by violating the sovereignty of Hungary, they wished away that of the Soviets.

Everything is clear: in Central Europe the de-Stalinizers insisted on continuing Stalin's policy when, already, their attitude in the U.S.S.R. and their own declarations were making it impossible; these contradictions, their ill-will, their half-concessions finally provoked the worst and justified the Stalinists. The latter, on temporarily retaking power, launched themselves on a policy, chancy, lazy and bloody, based on the distrust of man and of human life; they artificially provoked the return of the cold war in order to establish their strength on fear. From this perspective, the Russian intervention in Hungary takes on all its meaning: it is a localized operation in the framework of a cold war which has not yet broken out. Now war suspends all legality, socialist or not: thus the sole justification of the Budapest coup is the obviousness of war; the blood spilled in Hungary is only a small stream compared to the torrents of blood which are going to flow.

Blood will not flow. Neither the Americans nor the Russians desire hot war; the cold war is out-of-date. Neo-Stalinism goes against history. It finds its only justification—and even that is only apparent—in the Peoples Democracies which Stalin ruined; elsewhere, everything contradicts it: the new Russian society, the existence of a Communist China, the very attitude of the West. This abstract and insane realism is totally unreal: it has compromised the U.S.S.R. in the eyes of the world without managing to subdue Hungary. It must be condemned because the facts condemn it and opposed by the only policy which today is adapted to reality: that which makes of man the measure of everything and which combats all alienations, even when they are improperly decked out with the title of "socialism"; that which prefers in every case negotiation to violence and reasoned solutions to massacres; that which refuses to take an option on future war and insists on preparing peace by acts of peace; that, finally, which will dare to reestablish the sovereignty of the people in the Soviet Union and the national sovereignty of the "satellite" countries. This policy of confidence and expansion is precisely the one which one could have expected after the Twentieth Congress. Circumstances impose it: here it is called *democratization* and there *de-Stalinization*; but, whatever its name, there is no other possible road. The U.S.S.R. finds itself before an alternative which it can push back by a few massacres but not evade: either it will liquidate its Stalinist bureaucracy and of itself reconsider its relations with all the Peoples Democracies, or else their upheavals will throw it into local repressions which will end absurdly by unleashing this world war which no one wants and which they will have claimed to prevent.

Merleau-Ponty writes in *L'Express*: "One can speak equitably about the U.S.S.R., but only if it chooses to come back into the ranks of history and if one *does not believe in it*, either as Good or as Evil, if one has given up fetishes." That seems obvious. Still we must know where that leads us. Now, he also says: "The only correct attitude is then to see communism in the relative, as a fact without any privilege, as an undertaking tormented by its own contradiction, which glimpses it, and which must go beyond it." It is on this point that we cannot be in agreement with him: certainly, we have indicated, right here, that the building of socialism was "tormented by its own contradictions"; if it wasn't thus, history would stop. But it is true also that these contradictions are engendered right out of the undertaking itself and that the latter cannot be understood outside of its objectives. It intends to give liberty and justice to all men; it is not this fundamental intention which can wrench it out of history since, quite to the contrary, it is in and through history that it intends to be realized. But no more is needed to distinguish it radically from all policies which aim to establish or to preserve the domination of a class over the whole of society. Each socialist nation is a singular undertaking which aims at constructing a world with the means at hand: one will understand nothing of Peoples China if one doesn't first of all see in it and find in it, in the smallest detail, the concerted effort of six hundred million men to suppress misery and hunger. In which bourgeois democracy will one find this élan towards the future, this conscious and sustained action, this living unity? It cannot be a question of identifying the U.S.S.R. with the Good nor the declarations of *Pravda* with Absolute Truth: nothing can replace, in the East any more than in the West, these successive approximations, these debates, these dialogues which allow—slowly, progressively— Truth to be brought into the clear. But, willy-nilly, socialist construction *is privileged in this*: that one must, to understand it, espouse its movement and adopt its objectives; in a word, one judges what it does in the name of what it intends, its means in the name of its end, whereas one evaluates all other undertakings by what they ignore, what they neglect or what they reject. This privilege explains another: only those who participate, in the East and in the West, in the movement of socialism can and should judge. Merleau-Ponty seems to appeal implicitly to some eagle's nest from which one would evaluate jointly the evolution of peoples regimes and that of capitalist democracies. To which it is necessary to respond: either this transcendent point of view does not exist, or else it is socialism itself, not as an absolute principle, soaring above the mêlée, but as an historic reality, concrete, positive and total. But the immense privileges of this undertaking must be paid for by the extreme severity of its judges, that is to say of its own artisans. To become indignant against bourgeois colonialism is to waste one's time: we know what the system is and we know who Mr. Borgeaud is; everything is so clear and so long since, that anger seems to me at least optional. It is less a matter of condemning than of eliminating. On the other hand, when Soviet policy puts socialism in danger, contradicts its principles and its goals, when the means which it uses risk destroying the ends its serves, we will reserve all of our indignation for it. It is no longer a question of fighting an enemy nor of eliminating a system: it is necessary to condemn a method and the leaders who are applying it. The grandeur of their undertaking and the weight of their responsibilities deprive them *in all cases of all extenuating circumstances*. The despicable acts of the *colons*, the capitalist exploitation can have reduced men and nations to despair: the proletariats and the colonized peoples have forged their hopes in the face of them, crimes and massacres will change nothing. But when Russian tanks fire on the buildings of Budapest, when they transform, as Césaire so well says, socialism into a nightmare, when the State police arrest and deport the Hungarian youth and the workers, it is men's hope—their only hope—which is brought back into question. A young Russian, in a conversation which a French friend reported to me, began by accepting criticisms in good grace and by admitting the defects of the regime. But after a moment, he asked, irritated: "And you? what else do you have to offer us?" My friend made the response which we all would have made: "Nothing. The West has nothing to offer." But it is necessary to add today: "And you Russians, if you succeeded in making us believe that your barbarity in Budapest is only a normal episode of socialist construction, no one in the world would have anything to offer any more. To anyone." And I particularly notice, as a matter of fact, that Merleau-Ponty doesn't get very upset over the Soviet intervention: if the U.S.S.R. is worth neither more nor less than capitalist England, then, indeed, not much is left to us but to cultivate our garden. In order to preserve hope, precisely the opposite must be done: to recognize, through and beyond errors, monstrosities and crimes, the obvious privileges of the socialist camp and to condemn with all the more force the policy which endangers these privileges.

"WAS THIS REALLY THE MOMENT? . . ."

And now the U.S.S.R. is condemned! That will provoke smiles: "If you knew to what an extent it doesn't give a damn!" Do I know it! We are hundreds of thousands, in Paris, who consider the Suez affair to be a piracy and who don't digest the Budapest affair very well. Do we count? Wouldn't a half ration of a Bulganin rocket be enough to plunge us all together into a lasting silence? How claim, after that, that our protests are not idealistic?

Nevertheless, I am not sure that they remain without effect. On the U.S.S.R., of course, we can have no effect: we must have confidence in its workers, in its students, in those who, within the apparatus, struggle for the elimination of Stalinism. But there is in France a Party which would not escape the guided missiles any more than we and whose enthusiasm would be wiped off the earth at the same instant as our protests. It is directed by a Political Bureau which congratulated the Russians on their felicitous initiative and a member of which, recently, proclaimed himself quite "cheered up" by these exemplary massacres. That Party is our business, we know it well; we have all been, for a shorter or longer time, its fellow travelers: it is on it that we must, that we can effectively act. And here I am right back with my correspondents. There is one, among them, whom I annoy profoundly. He's a progressive. It's not that he disapproves of my opinion; he goes so far as to confide in me that he shares it: but he, at least, had the courage to keep quiet and he considers it regrettable that I lacked this courage: "Was this really the moment? The anticommunist hysteria is at its height, the crimes of our Government deprive us of the right to condemn anyone whatsoever; we have only one task: to unite against the Algerian war." Sir, if this is not the moment, say right away that the moment will never come. For, finally, suppose that the Russians, tomorrow, invade Poland and deport Gomulka: the anticommunist hysteria would take on such a violence that it would be more than ever necessary to close ranks around the Party. And if, the day after tomorrow, some Migs bombarded Bucharest? This time all hell would break loose and I think that you would sign up, were you to die a little later from suppressed irritation.

I get you: these shouts, these torches, these arsonists, lynchers, ugly mugs, all this sadism in full light, the noble indignation of Messrs. Tixier-Vignancour and Biaggi; I agree with you that it's repugnant. And I know too that they tried to take advantage of the occasion to dissolve the C.P., that they're still thinking of it and that our Prime Minister, if the Right's pack closes in too closely one day, will try to divert its rage by throwing it the anticommunist bone to gnaw on. Bourdet said it and we are numerous who repeat it: that day, Mr. Mollet will find the entire Left drawn up against him. That said, I tell you flatly that we will no longer be had by blackmail fascist-style. Recall: a few Communist intellectuals had joined in a moderate protest against the Soviet intervention in Hungary. After the riot, the leaders of the C.P. accused them of having contributed—"in fact," of course, and not "by intention"—to provoking it. Well, that also, you see, is repugnant. The dead and wounded Communists were used against their comrades. The U.S.S.R. has been mistaken a hundred times, its chiefs have publicly admitted it; however, if you don't enthusiastically accept its new errors, you are objectively an assassin. Naturally, this is only talk: the petitioners weren't hanged. But the Party isn't in power: recall the Slanskys, Rajks, Kostovs. That began often by a guilt in fact; the intention came some time afterwards, then the confession, then the rope. Everyone knows nevertheless that Mr. Biaggi's gangs were on deck: do you really believe that these fine gangsters, in order to begin their work, were waiting for the benediction of three militants of the extreme Left whose very names they didn't even know? Do you see them throwing themselves into the fray shouting "J.-F. Rolland with us"? When we were denouncing the Indochinese war, we were stabbing French soldiers in the back; when we condemn Soviet aggression, we are opening the door to fascism and are putting the finger on the best militants for the killers. The process doesn't vary: whatever the truth, there is always something much more important which must be preferred to it: the morale of the troops or the nation, the unity of a party, the honor of the family, in a word, the Holy. The duty

123

of the patriot, the citizen, the militant, is to peddle pious lies: one keeps them on one's tongue like a communion wafer and then one passes them off to a neighbor, sanctimoniously. What good does it do? From time to time the sewer bursts—Khrushchev's report, for example—and these blessed peddlers get all the crap at once. Wouldn't it have been better to retail it?

And then, believe me, these disturbances will not be repeated: a fascist demonstration may cause deaths, damage buildings; it can't shake the Party: the Party has been there before; it knows how to profit from them, on the contrary; the militants tighten ranks, dissensions are forgotten. The Right quickly understood that it was on a wrong track. The newspapers at first beamed on these proud French youths who were laying siege to a handful of men cornered in the building at the Châteaudun intersection; and then, beginning the next day they corrected the range: *Le Figaro* itself deplored the impetuousness, the *furia francese* of these "students." And the National Assembly? With what promptness it took a position against the dissolution of the C.P.! What a majority: 453 votes against 81! It wasn't love, however, which was firing them up; but the deputies were saying to each other: "Let's not make martyrs: they'll sink by themselves." So? Why should I keep quiet? You say that the Algerian war must be our first, our constant concern: that's true. But the Party returns the Right's courtesy; the Right served it by its violence, it is serving the Right by its pious lies: he who finds it quite natural that Russian soldiers fire on Hungarian workers, by what right would he become indignant when French soldiers fire on Arab peasants? You have anticipated the objection, you write me: "One cannot compare. . . . It's not the same thing." Naturally, it's not the same thing: but it's no longer even a question of the truth here, I am speaking to you about the efficacy of a campaign. The Communist orator who responds before a peoples' gathering to his critics from the Right: "One can't compare, it's not the same thing!" you know very well will have his back against the wall and he will have lost the game. That's why, if there is still time, the only way of helping the Communist Party to get back its credit is to oppose the truth to its lies, as often, as long as it is necessary in order that all its militants be convinced. A few months ago, in Budapest, a Hungarian newspaperwoman denounced the outrageous comfort the high officials enjoyed. The article was reproduced in the British press and Rakosi blew up: was she seeking scandal, did she want to feed imperialist propaganda? She answered simply: "The scandal is your luxury; it is not what I say about it." That's what I would willingly respond to Messrs. Fajon, Stil and Guyot: it is true that I consider their lies scandalous and that I say so. But I am not revealing anything to anybody: anyone can buy *L'Humanité* and judge it first hand. Ah! If I claimed that Mr. Stil, one night, in an obscure Montmartre alley, was an accomplice in an assassination, I would be making a gratuitous slander which might well injure him: but everyone knows, from his own articles, that he went to Budapest, that he saw Hungarian Democracy assassinated there and that he declared himself to be satisfied. So why should I restrain myself? I can say nothing worse about him than what he has said, do nothing meaner than to invite people to read him. When the Soviet leaders lie to their people, I cannot excuse them, but I can understand them: they're in the thick of it; entangled in their internal struggles, paralyzed by their ideology, caught in the trap of a "pacification" which endlessly calls for new violence: even if, suddenly, the de-Stalinizers won out, the officials would have to be put in prison or the lies continued to prevent the dislocation of the apparatus. But when André Stil calmly publishes his claptrap in these same columns in which others have put some out on Rajk, the camps, the "criminals in white blouses," when he gets back, after so many denials and slaps in the face, after the rehabilitation of so many innocent people whom he covered with his spit, to the same tone of serene infallibility and fulsome optimism, the reader is obliged to say to himself: "He's not in the thick of it; the French leaders aren't in the thick of it." I know and I approve the close friendship which ties them to the Russians: but, in the final count, they are responsible only before the working masses of their country. They will be considered all the more inexcusable since nothing prevents their speaking the truth and everything constrains them to do so. They certainly were not being asked for a violent condemnation of the Soviet intervention. No, but only to enlighten the opinions of their militants and of readers, to explain, to take their distance, not to smear themselves right off with blood which they haven't even spilled. What drove them to make themselves the accomplices of this distant crime when they could with a word clear themselves of it? Did they have to drag with them into disgrace the militants who had confidence in them? Was it really necessary to insult the victims before they knew anything? Couldn't they avoid revealing to all eyes the indigence of their Marxism and the poverty of their knowledge to the point of scandalizing the historians in their own Party? What! They were made to believe, for ten years, that the moon was made of green cheese; after which, one fine day, they were brutally informed that they had been had. Idle lesson, they learned nothing and forgot nothing; only just recently, the Soviet leaders had taken it on themselves to put them on their guard: the day after Poznan, Khrushchev talked of fascism and imperialism, he attributed the disturbances to foreign agents; the Polish Government denied it on the spot and the Russian newspapers, without abandoning their thesis, muted it and, in the end, breathed not another word about it. It was like a dress rehearsal of the Hungarian tragedy: the roles and the points of view were known in advance; everybody could foresee it, if Budapest rose up, Khrushchev would point out the presence in Hungary of fascist commandos and the Arrow Cross and Nagy would reveal to the world that the entire people supported the insurrection. Nothing doing: on the appointed day, the Political Bureau of the French C.P. saw rolling towards them a big green cheese; its members all cried out: "What a beautiful moon!" and this cry reverberated from one hundred and eighty thousand throats. That's why I say to my correspondent: yes, it is the moment, it is certainly the moment, perhaps it's even too late! For things to have come to that point, for the same error, ten times denounced, to spring up again, with the same unlikelihood, and be proclaimed truth, the French C.P. must be really sick; if it doesn't use the lance, gangrene will set in. Let Messrs. Duchet, Bidault, Tixier-Vignancour rejoice! But the men of the Left will not rejoice: by the votes it receives the C.P. remains the foremost party of France: rotten, it will pass on the clap to the whole Left.

What in fact can noncommunist movements and groups do? To unite *without the C.P.* is to condemn oneself to impotence; *against it* is to open the door to fascism. One solution remains, just one: unity of action *with it*; now it's precisely that one which the Party's policy makes impossible. For after all, no one is misled on this score, the Common Front of the Left, whatever the importance of the small political formations, will never be realized without a lasting understanding between the two great workers' parties. This is what we have not ceased to repeat here for the last ten years, it's what we will continue to repeat. Only a Popular Front can save our country: it alone can cure our colonial cancers, wrest the economy from stagnation, give it a new impetus, organize, under workers' control, mass production to raise the French standard of living; it alone can lay the bases of a social democracy, reconquer national sovereignty, break the Atlantic Bloc and put French power at the service of world peace. This policy, the only one which serves all the interests of France, the only one which can avoid for us bloody upheavals, fascism and perhaps civil war, neither of the two parties is strong enough to conduct without the other. But there is worse: neither of the two parties can pull itself out of the crisis it is going through without the other. The S.F.I.O. has got quite gray during the last ten years: the average age of its deputies, even that of its militants continues to rise. The C.P. is aging also; more slowly. It recruits less and less among the young; at the top, the apparatus is not being renewed. The rivalries, the fratricidal combats, the mutual hatred of these two venerable parties, all has ended up in sclerosis. Their degeneration is such that both are criminals (the Government of Mr. Guy Mollet throws itself into a war of aggression alongside of the British Conservatives; the leaders of the Communist Party publicly approve the arrests and deportations of workers) and each one uses the crimes of the other to justify its own. Now, when one goes around yelling: "Suez!" and the other: "Budapest!" they are perhaps leading their militants on, but by this reciprocal disqualification they throw discredit on the entire Left. It is certainly necessary to admit that our two great parties are the most despised in the world: the representative of the S.F.I.O., Mr. Commin, was booed out of an international meeting of Social-Democratic parties. Mr. Stil cut a poor figure in Poland, even poorer in Budapest; at the Congress of the Italian

128

C.P., Duclos was coolly received. This degeneration expresses that of the country: in a France asphyxiated by employers who are Malthusians of long-standing, social layers have been stratified, nothing changes, nothing budges; elsewhere, the up-heavals of industrial production entail such population trans-formations and the latter such changes in the workers' world that the union organs and political apparatuses must change in order to adapt; with us, economic stagnation has produced a profound split in the very heart of the proletariat; this split, politicians and union leaders exploit in turn: they live off it, their limited and shortsighted views reflect it. It is not a matter only of the faults of a team: the faults, the mutual hatred ex-press hardened contradictions. And yet, this broken, paralyzed Left, one half of which sinks into isolation, and the other half plays the game of right-wing politics, it is in it we place our last hope. Let it fall a little bit lower, it's fascism for us. Let it pick itself up and unite, let it overcome its internal contra-dictions, France can live. One must bet on it, no matter what happens: the Popular Front or paralysis, we must choose.

It's here that my correspondent goes on: "And you really believe that we will contribute to pasting these two disparate halves together again by flaying out at both of them?" Yes, I believe so. "If we must whack," he says, "let's whack at the Socialist Party: it's well-known that its leaders won't have any-thing to do with unity. But the C.P.? What does it say daily? That a United Front is necessary! Look at them: from Thorez to the bottom militant, they're holding out their hands to Guy Mollet, to Daniel Mayer, to Lacoste. Isn't that just what you want?" No, not exactly. Of course I can see that the C.P. is calling for unity of action but it goes about it in such a way that it makes it impossible. Let's look at it closely.

Since the election, the C.P. has consistently followed the

same policy. It was a question, in sum, of attaining on the national level the objectives which the U.S.S.R. is pursuing in the international domain; it was necessary to reassure, to contribute to the détente, to extend the zones of Communist influence by the realization of a common front of the workers' parties. This policy was dictated to the U.S.S.R. by the real de-Stalinization of Soviet society: it expressed the "thaw," the need for expansion of this formidable power. In France, it could have sense only if it was accompanied by a real de-Stalinization of the Party, that is to say, by democratization and a real expansion. What had to change, in a word, was the internal structure of the C.P., its relationship to the masses, its relations with the other political and social groups. It had to give and take, it had to give in order to take; it had to be sufficiently sure of itself—in the cultural domain, among others—to conquer and assimilate. Unfortunately the Party kept its Stalinist structure, its Stalinist leadership: the policy of expansion was in contradiction with its profound distrust and its retractile attitude. The C.P. is today neither a party of the masses nor entirely a party of cadres. This formation of 180,000 militants, rather than expanding like the Italian C.P., has preferred to tighten ranks, to leave the working class outside. Since 1948, the Communist leaders have bet on war: the Atlantic Bloc would become more aggressive from day to day; on the eve of the conflict, the French Government would dissolve the Party; they wished to remain on the alert, a quick and trained group, which would not be hindered by large numbers and which would go underground without hindrance. Stalinization and the reduction of the C.P.s in France and Central Europe took place between Marshall's first offers and the second condemnation of Tito. Here as there, this contraction had the effect of cutting the Party off from the masses: it lost the means to influence them by taking away from them the means to control it. Five million voters vote for it every four years but these votes can't pass for a control: these electors give their votes "to the party which is the furthest to the Left," which doesn't imply that they approve all its policy: a vote is always more or less a compromise. The result of this transformation is two-fold: *first of all*, to the extent that it satellized the Party, it "parliamentarized" it, willy-nilly. It is not in the factory nor in the street that it carries off its victories: it is in the voting booth, on election day. Its strength tends to be reduced to the number of its deputies, its action seems to have efficacy only on the parliamentary level. But, in reality, the maneuvers of the other parties and, in particular, the Socialist betrayal have for immediate effect the disarming of its power: whatever the starting majority, another is formed almost immediately whose only goal is to neutralize it. What has it got? Germany is being rearmed, fighting goes on in Algeria, prices are rising. Against the Franco-British expedition, the Laborites have stirred up half of England. And we, what have we done? What have the one hundred and fifty Communist deputies done? What has the Party done with its five million votes? One can say that it has put them on ice. It weighs on political life with an enormous weight but that means only that the people in the majority decide on their vote *taking into account the Party's existence*. On the other hand, its obvious importance and its secret isolation have as effect to maintain and to reinforce the dictatorship of the Political Bureau: the sudden irruption of the masses could distend the cadres or make them burst apart, but this little petrified system, inefficient and uncontrollable, cannot be changed either by its own action or by the reaction of others. This situation naturally pushed it to seek the socialist alliance on the parliamentary plane since the

S.F.I.O. votes joined to its own would give it a real efficacy without modifying its structure: union from the bottom, to the contrary, would have led it to open up, to let itself be penetrated in order to penetrate in its turn, to let it replace the fixed borders which cut it off from the world by a somewhat fluid transitional zone where Socialists and Communists would have mingled in a kind of indistinctness. I do not think that there is room to speak, as Hervé does, of rightist opportunism and leftist opportunism: these notions no longer have exactly the same meaning since Stalin's death. But I will say rather that the structure of the C.P. was in flagrant contradiction with its policy: in consequence the latter necessarily had to remain inoperative and unreal.

The Fourteenth Congress profits from the Twentieth Soviet Congress to give a theoretical form to the general line adopted by the Political Bureau. Chapter 5 of the theses stresses "the possibilities of peacefully transforming the capitalist economy into a socialist economy." But, if one rejects armed insurrection and civil war, it is not only so that *internal* détente comes to the support of international détente. It is also because this theoretical change permits substituting for unity from the bottom, unity from the top. In fact, the alliance of the proletariat and the middle classes "will transform Parliament itself, from an instrument of bourgeois dictatorship into a tool of the popular will."

This thesis has been much criticized. But it is wrongly that it is considered reformist. In fact, it is not a matter of obtaining, thanks to universal suffrage, a continuous succession of improvements which would imperceptibly lead to the disappearance of capitalism: the Popular Front, carried to power by the votes of peasants, workers and intellectuals, will have to realize, in a dictatorial manner, the radical transformation of society. The Revolution, as an abrupt passing from a dying regime to the beginning of a new regime, will be accomplished on the taking of power. Only it will have lost its violent character. I don't think either that the thesis is in contradiction, as has been claimed, with the resolution of the Second Congress of the Communist International. In the latter, in fact, one reads: "Communism refuses to see in parliamentarianism one of the forms of future society. It sets itself as a goal the abolition of parliamentarianism. There can be no question of the utilization of bourgeois governmental institutions except with the view to their destruction." The Fourteenth Congress doesn't deny it: it specifies that parliamentarianism can, in present conditions, become the means of taking power. But it is very careful not to say what the revolutionary Front will do with the power when it has won it; nothing proves that its first act will not be to suppress Parliament.

What is less theoretical and much more serious is that the new statements confirm the disastrous practice of the C.P.: "Since the votes of our parliamentary groups mingle in the Assembly National, why not facilitate their task by acting in common through the country?"[1] In this surprising text it is not the profound unity of interests or conditions which militates in favor of a regrouping of the two parties of the Left; the Socialist worker is not told that he is in the same boat as his Communist comrade and, whether he likes it or not, engaged in the same struggle. No, but *since* the parliamentary groups vote in the same manner, the workers who elected these groups, whatever their divergences of view, elsewhere, will profit by getting together. It is the affiliation at the top which legitimizes the rapprochement at the base. Nothing less Marxist. And then the argument has no effect: especially in France,

---

[1] XIV Congress, address to Socialist comrades.

where, by tradition, the worker distrusts his deputy. But it is made *to have no effect*: its a matter only of favoring an electoral realignment which permits sending a leftist majority to the Assembly. The true milieu of the rapprochement is Parliament itself; all these theoretical considerations have as their goal persuading the Socialist Government to officially accept Communist support. That's what explains how Thorez could say recently that it was necessary "to win over the Socialist Party in its entirety to unity of action." At the base, one could try to detach the socialist Left from Mr. Mollet's party. In the Assembly, it's Mr. Mollet who reigns: over his group and over the country. He is the "Socialist Party in its entirety." It's with him that one must get along.

It's with him, precisely, that the C.P. will *never* get along. There's no question about it: the anticommunism of the Socialists is nowhere more virulent than in the parliamentary group. In the factories, in the government services, workers are tied together first by work and demands; the parliamentary group, closed in on itself, is separated from the Communist group by an unbridgeable gap. Fear dominates. And hatred. When a S.F.I.O. deputy thinks of the terrible misadventures of the Social-Democratic parties in the Peoples Democracies his hair stands on end; he gets purple with rage when he thinks that his colleagues of the C.P. consider him quite simply a traitor and that their smiles, their tender glances conceal a distrust which is never off guard. But these big feelings would be as nothing: there are the little ones. The electoral rivalries have considerable importance: each time that the C.P. and the S.F.I.O. have united, the C.P. got the best of it. The S.F.I.O. has fiefdoms, it wants to keep them. The result is that the policy of the C.P. resembles a gracious and monotonous ballet: the Faun runs after the Nymph and never catches her.

134

Guy Mollet is humored and Guy Mollet won't pay any attention. He rejects Communist votes or picks them up with tweezers. The C.P. voted him special powers: immediately the Government turned toward the Right and thanked it. Hatred and the fear of falling into the hands of the Communist deputies tears him away from the Left and draws him towards the M.R.P., the Independents. He betrays, as Duverger says. Will the Party denounce this betrayal? Not at all: it is necessary, isn't it, to leave the door open. *L'Humanité* complains melancholicly: on the eve of the elections, it was hoping for other tomorrows; the parliamentary group abstains when it is sure that Mollet will have his majority. Algeria is spoken about, of course: but with moderation. In order not to lose face, the Party press grumbles a bit. But it is understood that they will not rock the boat. The Peace Movement, very active at the time of Mr. Bidault and the war in Vietnam, has fallen by the wayside: no national campaign, no meetings, no "days of action"; its militants complain, some resign: they are not held back. As for the working class, the result and perhaps the goal of this policy is that it is totally demobilized: nothing which resembles the strikes of the dockers of Marseille, the demonstrations for the freeing of Henri Martin. The workers are disgusted by the Algerian war but they are left without instructions, without marching orders. The C.P. harvests what it has sown: when it needs the masses, it no longer finds them. The failure of the counter-demonstration, November 13, does not signify simply nor even primarily that the C.G.T. workers condemned the Soviet intervention[1]; it is first of all the mark of a kind of disorientation: the working class is abandoned to the forces of massification. Disconcerted, the Frenchmen of the

---

[1] The setback of the C.G.T. in the union elections is a clearer indication of their disapproval.

Left don't know what to say. "This Algerian war," some of them think, "if Guy Mollet wages it and if Thorez lets it be done, perhaps it is just after all?" Some Socialists also, honest and timorous folk of the S.F.I.O., when they read *L'Humanité*, say: "Lots of noise for nothing." That reassures them: a popular movement would have encouraged them, constrained them perhaps to oppose the government; but this verbal violence, immediately eaten away by silence, gives them a clear conscience at little cost. During this time, 500,000 young men are wasting their time in Algeria, if not their health or their lives, the economy is flat on its face, some workers are unemployed three days out of seven. There's the result of this Ballet of the Lefts, where one of the two parties wishes to embrace the other who avoids it by taking off to the right.

And yet, two months ago, discouraged by the inanities of Guy Mollet, some Socialist deputies on their own had got to the point of playing with the idea of a new Popular Front. It is then that the leaders of the C.P. rendered a signal service to the Head of the Government: they happily approved the Budapest slaughter. Truly, Mr. Guy Mollet wasn't hoping for so much; but he fully took advantage of his luck and provoked without too much clumsiness "the anticommunist hysteria." Those who were struck by it first of all were the very same ones who were thinking, just the day before, about drawing nearer to the C.P.; these Socialists went mad: with joy because they had barely escaped, with rage because they had run deadly perils. I even think there were a few of them, mature gentlemen, who were all for marching on the Soviet Embassy. Was the Political Bureau even aware that it ruined for years the chances for a Single Front? Did it ever believe these chances existed? It's not I who will decide.

You who ask if it is really the moment to speak, consider this monstrous Party which blocks and freezes five million votes, demobilizes the working class, abandons mass action for parliamentary maneuver, feebly denounces the Algerian war in order to humor—completely in vain—the Socialists and doesn't hesitate, at the same moment, to justify their distrust by senseless statements on the Hungarian events; tell yourself that its attitude is no longer even that of unconditional surrender to the U.S.S.R. but that its leaders fake, cut down Soviet texts or postpone their publication; that they hide or minimize the progress of de-Stalinization *even in the U.S.S.R.*, and that they highly praise any policy inspired by the ghost of Stalin; keep in mind that these same leaders no longer limit themselves to accepting the decisions of the Soviet Union but that they boast of influencing them; that they lean on the most Stalinist segment of the apparatus and thus contribute to reinforcing its influence and, as a consequence, to slowing down democratization everywhere; remember, finally, that so many errors and faults, so much destruction have had as goal and as effect to petrify, in the C.P., certain anachronistic structures, valuable in the time of the cold war but which condemn it today to inefficiency; weigh carefully these errors which can be mortal and tell me if it is not time, if it is not high time that the partisans of the United Front publicly denounce the obstacles which retard its constitution. Understand me: it is necessary to work also on the Socialist Party. But the Socialist attitude is determined by the policy of the C.P.: never will the militants of the S.F.I.O. get rid of the fear which is gnawing them as long as the C.P. remains this prehistoric monster, at once, terrible and impotent: for, they well know it's their betrayal which reduces it to impotence and, if they draw near to it, it will suddenly take on again its virulence. They feel *relative*: their Party has only three million voters and then, above all, the events in Central Europe lead them to believe that they will be gobbled up. One will be able to dissipate their fears and their loathings only to the extent that one influences the C.P. first of all. In India, the caste system engendered insurmountable contradictions at all levels of society but Gandhi judged it useless to take them all into consideration: "It was necessary," he thought, "to find the kingpin of the structure and to concentrate one's efforts on it alone": it is well-known that he found it without difficulty: it was very simply the caste of pariahs. Likewise, to break up the stratifications which threatened to transform the French Left into a system of castes, one must first of all influence the proud pariahs of our society, the Communist untouchables. Let them change *first*, the whole works is saved.

1. The C.P. would have taken away every pretext from Mr. Mollet's anticommunist propaganda if it had broadly and honestly informed the readers of *L'Huma*, if rather than recopying servilely the Soviet version, it had given its militants the means to arrive at an opinion, if, instead of maladroitly publishing its distrust of the masses, its spokesman, Mr. Fajon, had made an effort really to analyze the situation in Hungary. It will be said that I'm dreaming, that that wasn't possible, that the U.S.S.R. would not have tolerated it. That's true. Or rather, it's true *in France*; wasn't Togliatti saying only yesterday: "What we cannot admit is a return to the past system—intervention in the internal questions of the parties . . . instigation of ruptures in other parties or in the workers' movement as a whole—never mind who suggests it. . . . We are against the return to any form of centralized organization (in the international domain)".[1] And then one must know

---

[1] Speech of December 9, 1956 to the VIII Congress of the Italian C.P. But the Italian C.P. was never cut off from the masses: its two million members give it its strength and its life, it finds in them a support and a control. The French C.P. remains up in the air.

what one wants: the Single Front or unconditional obedience to the U.S.S.R.; in any case it is impossible to run both hares at once. It would be absurd for the Party to cut itself off from the U.S.S.R. or to break with it; it is no less absurd for it to be unreservedly in subjection to it. When Stalin was alive, the Soviet Union was *the* truth: it isn't any longer; the Twentieth Congress showed beneath the false evidence of Stalinism a collection of lies, errors and faults; how would one require of a fraternal party that it reject the infallibility of Stalin to grant it forthwith to Khrushchev? Moreover, the U.S.S.R. is not *the error* either: it is a nation which is in the process of making itself, which flounders about in the contradictions of socialism, whose leaders sometimes see much further than we and other times much less far. The time of revealed truths of the gospel has passed: a Communist Party can live in the West, only if it acquires the right of free examination. Don't speak of Titoism: the French Party isn't in power yet. It's a question only of laying down a principle: the Communist Party is responsible only before the working class of its country. And of conforming to it. From this follows necessarily for the U.S.S.R. the obligation to treat the western parties on an equal footing. If the French leaders explain to the Soviet leaders that the United Front has this price tag, won't the latter be encouraged to reconsider their relationships with our C.P.? This loosening of international ties, this abandoning of "centralism," isn't it in line with a policy of influence and expansion? Straight information (which doesn't mean "objective"), a correct and honest evaluation, sovereignty of the working class, equality in relations with the U.S.S.R., everything holds together. Without this first condition, the French Left is dead, the Party is mummified.

2. The Single Front remains unattainable as long as the C.P. persists in seeking it at the top through the agreement of

parliamentary groups. It is by the base that it will be made, if it is to be made one day. But, as I pointed out earlier, as long as the Party keeps the tight structure of a persecuted group, threatened with dissolution and which is preparing to go underground again, it is completely unsuitable for carrying out this vast fermentation which must produce Unity some day. Its watertight compartments[1] result today in separating the militants into heterogeneous groups of workers, petits bourgeois, intellectuals: this diversity of training, of interests, of background calls for and legitimizes the dictatorial authority of the apparatus; the isolation of the groups facilitates it. It is necessary to break down these structures of distrust, to multiply the contacts of the militants with each other if one wants to be able some day to re-establish those of the militants with the masses. The organization of the C.P., perfectly adapted to underground action, is incapable of assuring by itself alone the broad and vital action of an officially recognized party. To the extent that official tolerance can, from one day to the next, give place to persecutions, this structure in networks must remain. But it must be compensated by the multiplication of exchanges and contacts; the terrible accusation "of factional activity" (d'activité fractionnelle) reinforces the compartmentalization, it is it which makes terror reign which prevents communication between men and the circulation of ideas. One can condemn, like Lenin, factional activity on the condition that the "tendencies" have a way to manifest themselves in the

---

[1] The intellectuals have no contact with the workers. The students militate in student cells, professors in lycée cells, the presence of the bell ringer or the dining-hall waiter could not after all count as a direct contact with the industrial proletariat. The writers, who live in general in bourgeois neighborhoods, frequent petits bourgeois in the neighborhood cell. The party officials gladly reap benefit from the distrust which the intellectuals inspire in the manual workers. Even in the meetings of the Peace Movement the "hair-splitter" is opposed to the "door-to-door militant."

140

organism of the Party. But there is no doubt today that the tendencies become factions because they cannot be expressed in the institutional framework of the C.P. Factions will be avoided only by encouraging *on every level* criticism and discussions. Reduced to silence in the organized groups, condemned if he expresses himself outside of them, the militant of this party of the masses is in reality completely alone vis-a-vis its direction, and his isolation reflects the isolation of the C.P. If the C.P. wants to regain the support of the working masses, it must accept their control. As long as the elements of the base communicate only through the top, the C.P. will remain closed. If it wishes to weld itself to the masses, to give unity back to them and to find life again through them, it must become decompressed. It is this very operation, based on a policy of expansion, which we can call democratization. This is not the moment to examine under what form the C.P. can accept the revival of tendencies: even if the leaders themselves would wish to encourage them, the ossification of the structures would not allow them to be expressed; this crucial question is therefore subordinate to the modifications which the Party must bring to its own constitution if it wishes to become a mass party again and to impose from the base this United Front which the S.F.I.O. persists in rejecting.

Equality in relationships with the U.S.S.R., accuracy of information, democratization, renewal of contact with the masses and their mobilization, *first of all* against the Algerian war: such are the necessary conditions for the resuscitation of the C.P., for the realization of a Common Front by the two great workers' parties. Between the two things, I don't make a distinction. Every "Left" has its problems: ours is that of workers' unity. It would be as abstract to consider the C.P. outside of this concrete situation as to envisage it without taking into account its ties with the U.S.S.R. For our part, it's been twelve years that we have been debating with the Communists. At first with violence, later in friendship. But our goal was always the same: to cooperate with our feeble forces in achieving this union of the Lefts which *alone* can still save our country. Today, we return to the opposition: for this very simple reason that there is no other position to take; alliance with the C.P. as it is, as it intends to remain, can have no other effect than to compromise the last chances of the United Front. Our program is clear: through and beyond a hundred contradictions, internal struggles, massacres, de-Stalinization is in process; it is the only effective policy which serves, in the present moment, socialism, peace, the rapprochement of the workers' parties: with our resources as intellectuals, read by intellectuals, we will try to help in the de-Stalinization of the French Party.

Glossary
and
Index

ARROW CROSS: principle extreme rightist movement in pre-World War II Hungary. *18, 51n, 127.*

AVOS: (Allamvédelmi Osztaly) Hungarian secret state security police. *19, 27, 46, 51, 52.*

BIAGGI, JEAN: b. 1918. Founder and President of the *Parti Patriote Populaire* (1957–1958) and co-founder of the *Rassemblement pour l'Algérie française* (1959). *122, 123.*

BIDAULT, GEORGES: b. 1899. President of the M.R.P. President of the Provisional Government (1946). Prime Minister (October 1949–June 1950). *127, 135.*

BLANQUI, LOUIS: (1805–1881) French socialist and revolutionary. Participated in the 1848 Revolution. *5.*

BORBA: Daily paper of the Yugoslav Communist Party. *65.*

BORGEAUD, HENRI: b. 1895. Senator from Algeria (1946–1959). Administrator of many Algerian companies. *8, 120.*

BOURDET, CLAUDE: b. 1909. Founder of the weekly *L'Observateur* (1952). (Now *Nouvel–Observateur*). Founder of the *Centre d'Action des Gauches Indépendents* (1952) which was absorbed by the *Nouvelle Gauche* in 1954 then by the *Union de la Gauche Socialiste* (1957). *69, 123.*

BOURSES DU TRAVAIL: Local labor exchanges and center of union activity formed from 1887 on and linked in a national federation in 1892. To be distinguished from *syndicats* (craft or industrywide unions). The *Fédération des Bourses du Travail* united with the C.G.T. in 1902.

BOUSSAC, MARCEL: b. 1889. Textile industrialist. *8.*

BURNHAM, JAMES: b. 1905. American. Author of *The Managerial Revolution. 14.*

CASANOVA, LAURENT: b. 1906. Member of the Central Committee of the French Communist Party and of its Political Bureau. Party spokesman on intellectuals. Deputy. *24, 25, 27–28, 37.*

---

*Glossary compiled by the translator. Identifications mostly are as of the time of the events referred to in the text.

CÉSAIRE, AIMÉ: b. 1913. Deputy from Martinique. In the Communist group of the Assembly until 1956 then in the *Groupe du Parti du Regroupement Africain et des Federalistes* (1958). *120.*

C.G.T.: *Confédération Générale du Travail.* Formed in 1895. After the 1902 pact with the *Fédération des Bourses* it acquired its present structure of two sections: the *Bourses* and the *Fédérations* (national trade unions). *37, 135.*

COMMIN, PIERRE: (1907–1958) Assistant general-secretary of the S.F.I.O. in 1947, member of the National Committee and acting general-secretary in 1956. *128.*

DUCHET, ROGER: b. 1906. Political Director of *France-Indépendante.* General-secretary of the *Centre National des Indépendants et des Paysans.* Minister (1951–1953). *9, 127.*

DUCLOS, JACQUES: b. 1896. President of the Communist Group in the National Assembly (1946–1958). *129.*

L'EXPRESS: weekly founded in 1953 by Jean-Jacques Servan-Schreiber which supported Pierre Mendès-France and favored negotiation in the Indochinese war. *11, 118.*

FAJON, ETIENNE: b. 1906. Deputy (1946–1958). Member of the Political Bureau of the Communist Party since 1945. Secretary of the Communist Party (1954–1956). Director of *l'Humanité.* *16, 22, 28, 125, 138.*

FEJTÖ, FRANÇOIS: formerly professor and journalist in Hungary. With *Agence France-Presse* since 1944. Author of *Tragédie hongroise. 54, 92n.*

LE FIGARO: founded in 1854 (daily in 1866). Conservative morning paper. Director: Louis-Gabriel Robinet. *124.*

FIGARO LITTÉRAIRE: weekly supplement of *Le Figaro.* Started in 1946. *11.*

FRANCE-NOUVELLE: weekly review of the Communist Party. founded in 1945. *20.*

FRANCE-SOIR: largest afternoon daily newspaper (circulation over one million). Moderate. Director: Pierre Lazareff. *11.*

GARAUDY, ROGER: b. 1913. Senator (1959). Member of the Political Bureau of the Communist Party. Deputy (1945–1951 and 1956–1958). Director of *Cahiers du Communisme*. Author of novels, political and philosophical works and a leading polemicist. *20, 22, 33, 38.*

GERÖ, ERNÖ: First secretary of the Hungarian Socialist Workers' Party after Rákosi's second dismissal (July 1956). *16, 17, 18, 19, 20, 44, 45, 49, 63n.*

GUESDE, JULES: (1845–1922) introduced Marxism to the French labor movement in 1872. Opposed the reformism of Jean Jaurès. *5.*

GUYOT, RAYMOND: b. 1903. Deputy. Senator (1946–1958). Member of the Political Bureau of the Communist Party. *125.*

HERVÉ, PIERRE: former editor of *L'Action*. Broke with the C.P. over Hungary. *132.*

HORTHY, ADMIRAL MIKLÓS: (1868–1957) Regent of Hungary (1920–1944). *11, 26n, 40, 55.*

HÔTEL MATIGNON: official residence and office of the French Prime Minister. *112.*

L'HUMANITÉ: (sometimes called *L'Huma*) daily newspaper founded in 1904 and directed by Jean Jaurès until 1914. Organ of the Communist Party since 1920. *1, 2, 20, 23, 24, 28, 53, 60, 125, 135, 136, 138.*

INDÉPENDENTS: name given the loosely organized party of French conservatives of liberal economic outlook. Nominally anti-Gaullist. Included former members of the *Alliance Démocratique*, *Républicains Indépendents, Parti Republicain de la Liberté* and the Peasant Party. *135.*

JAURÈS, JEAN: (1859–1914) Brilliant orator. Leader of the French Socialist Party. Director of *L'Humanité*. Assassinated in 1914. *8.*

KÁDÁR, JÁNOS: b. 1912. Former "national Communist." Prime Minister of Hungary (November 1956–January 1958) and First Secretary of the Socialist Workers' Party since 1957. *15, 19, 41, 42n, 63, 64.*

KOSTOV, TRAJCO: (1897–1949) Bulgarian Deputy Prime Minister. Tried in December 1949. Executed. Rehabilitated in 1956. *15, 123.*

LACOSTE, ROBERT: b. 1898. Socialist deputy (1946–1958). Resident Minister in Algeria (1956–1957). *114, 129.*

LANIEL, JOSEPH: b. 1889. Prime Minister (June 1953–June 1954). *5.*

DE LISSAGARY, PROSPER OLIVIER: (1839–1901) founded *Revue des cours littéraires* and *La Bataille*. Author of *Histoire de la Commune de Paris* (1876). *6.*

MALETER, PAL: General. Commander of the Hungarian resistance forces. Executed November 1956. *34.*

MARAT, JEAN-PAUL: (1743–1793) deputy to the Convention. Assassinated by Charlotte Corday. *52.*

MARTIN, HENRI: b. 1927. Received a 5-year sentence (October 1950) for distributing anti-Vietnam war leaflets among other sailors. *135.*

MAYER, DANIEL: b. 1909. General-secretary of the Socialist Party (1943–1946). Deputy (1946–1958). Member of the National Political Committee of the *Parti Socialiste Unifié* (1960). *129.*

MERLEAU-PONTY, MAURICE: (1908–1961) Professor of Philosophy at the *College de France*. Author. Founder with Jean-Paul Sartre and Simone de Beauvoir of *Les Temps Modernes*. Writer on *L'Express*. *89, 118, 120, 121.*

MOLLET, GUY: b. 1905. General-secretary of the Socialist Party (S.F.I.O.) since 1946. Prime Minister (January 1956–May 1957). *2, 3, 6, 7–8, 9, 10, 40, 114, 123, 128, 129, 134, 135, 136, 138.*

M.R.P.: *Mouvement Républicain Populaire.* Post-World War II

Catholic social party which accepted state economic intervention and nationalization of industries. *8, 135.*

NAGY, FERENC: b. 1903. Secretary-general of the Hungarian Smallholders Party (1930). Prime Minister (February 1946–May 1947). Exiled. Now in U.S.A. *35.*

NAGY, IMRE: (1895–1956) Communist Hungarian Prime Minister (July 1953–April 1955) and called again October 1956. Executed November 1956. *17, 19, 26n, 32, 37, 43, 44–45, 47–48, 49, 52, 57, 63, 85–86, 107, 127.*

OCHAB, GENERAL EDWARD: b. 1906. First Secretary of the Central Committee of the Polish United Workers' Party since 1956. *17.*

PETÖFI CIRCLE: (named after a revolutionary poet of 1848) a club of Hungarian writers, formed during the Nagy period, which drew in younger people. It openly demanded Nagy's return to power. *31.*

PRAVDA: official daily organ of the Communist Party of the Soviet Union. *17, 65, 119.*

RAJK, LÁSZLÓ: (1909–1949) the leading Hungarian "national Communist", former Minister of the Interior. Hanged October 1949. Rehabilitated 1956. *15, 24, 26, 51n, 108, 123, 126.*

RÁKOSI, MÁTYÁS: (1892–1963) First Secretary of the Hungarian Socialist Workers' Party until 1956. Prime Minister (August 1952–July 1953). *16, 19, 23, 26, 29n, 30, 31, 33, 40, 55, 60, 87, 89, 107, 108, 125.*

ROKOSSOVSKY, CONSTANTIN: b. 1896. Soviet Marshal born in Warsaw. Minister of Defense in Poland (1949–1956). *17.*

ROLLAND, JACQUES-FRANCIS: b. 1922. Communist. Joined Vercors, Sartre, Simone de Beauvoir and Louis de Villefosse in a letter denouncing the use of guns and tanks against the Hungarian people. Expelled from the C.P. *123.*

DE ROUGEMENT, DENIS: b. 1906. Swiss Director, *Centre Européen de la Culture*; Chairman Executive Committee, Congress for Cultural Freedom. Author. Professor at the *Institut Universitaire d'études Européenes* at Geneva, since 1963. *1, 2–3.*

SAINT-BARTHOLOMEW'S DAY MASSACRE: August 24, 1572, massacre of the Protestants in Paris. *53*.

SAINT-DENIS, SAINT-OUEN, BILLANCOURT: working class districts known as the Red Belt of Paris. *38, 112*.

S.F.I.O.: *Section Française de la Internationale Ouvrière* (Second International), the French Socialist Party founded in 1905. In 1920 the left wing majority seceded at the Congress of Tours to form the Communist Party. *7, 9, 128, 132, 134, 136, 137, 141*.

SLANSKY, RUDOLF: (1901–1952) former secretary-general of the Czechoslovakian Communist Party. Executed November 1952. *15, 51n, 123*.

SMALLHOLDERS' PARTY: potentially the most important Hungarian postwar political party, it drew its support from the peasants (more than half the population). The leaders were mostly middle class intellectuals, their views varying from liberal conservative to semi-socialist radicalism. Received 57% of the votes in the October 1945 elections. *30, 46, 48, 58*.

SOCIAL-DEMOCRATIC PARTY OF HUNGARY: founded in 1892. Divided by four factions in the postwar years: right wing, center, left independent, left pro-communist. Received 17% of the votes in 1947. Merged with the Communists to form the Hungarian Socialist Workers' Party (June 14, 1948). *30 32, 40, 42, 43, 46, 58, 109, 114*.

STIL, ANDRÉ: b. 1921. Communist. Editor-in-chief of *Ce Soir* (1949), of *L'Humanité* (1950–1959). Stalin Prize (1951). *15, 23, 35, 125–6, 128*.

THOREZ, MAURICE: (1900–1964) General Secretary of the Communist Party (1930–1964). *29n, 129, 134, 136*.

TIXIER-VIGNANCOUR, JEAN-LOUIS: b. 1907. right wing attorney. Deputy. President of the *Rassemblement national* (1954). *122, 127*.

WALDECK-ROCHET: (often listed as Rochet, Waldeck) Communist leader. Expert on agrarian questions. Replaced Thorez as general-secretary of the Communist Party in 1964. *19, 20, 22, 35*.